# A POET'S LIFE
# FOR ME

Henry Mulligan

First published 2023
by Rowanvale Books Ltd
The Gate
Keppoch Street
Roath
Cardiff
CF24 3JW
www.rowanvalebooks.com

A CIP catalogue record for this book is available from the British Library.
Hardback ISBN: 978-1-914422-71-3
Paperback ISBN: 978-1-914422-93-5
Ebook ISBN: 978-1-914422-92-8

# Contents

# Introduction

As I write this I have no publisher and, to be honest with you, more worryingly, no bloody book yet. I mean, who the hell is the target audience for poetry? Well, actually, I have a vague idea in my head, and I'm not liking who I'm seeing. I refrain from using the phrase 'comic poetry' as it makes me heave and not want to ever meet myself. But I plough on with the stuff because some ill-advised internal feeling says that there *are* people like *you* out there. I throw labels at you like good-humoured, mature, highbrow, whilst society labels you odd, problematic, a misfit. Whichever form you take, you're appreciated. I can't say what kind of journey we're going to go on as this book unfolds (I haven't properly planned the thing), but we're going to make sure we enjoy it together as we blast through the chaos at our own pace.

And with any luck, this book will be so poignant and significant, the next wave of culture coyotes will be calling for me to be removed from public life in ten to twenty years' time because it hurts their feelings (poetry can be so cutting). They'll be shouting "silence him!" and "he's a monster!" and "he's a danger to our children!" and I'll be shouting "it's only poetry!" and "oh fuck off!" I'll be forced either into silence or aligning myself with my public defenders on the political spectrum, doing rather tense TV interviews about freedom of speech with some censor-hungry lunatic making me sweat. It makes me wonder whether I'd just go down without a fight and really knuckle down. Write another book that'll win me a posthumous award. Really stick it to 'em after death. Live on in their sad little minds like a poison.

Perhaps if this book *is* published, I'll get to do a slightly easier TV interview someday, so I can evaluate my sweat levels on camera when no one's going for my throat. See how composed I am after getting up at four a.m. to be on a Sunday morning watchalong. Will I come across well in the interview? Will I be able to cook on live TV?

Will I have a blinding, *violent* row with the stylist about my look? These are all questions that need to be answered if I'm to choose between being silenced or swinging back from the ropes, but all in good time.

I suppose there's probably some old philosophical quote that sums this up a lot quicker, and I suppose it'd be this: talent has a price.

## Brian

Brian had boiled it with the lid open,
steaming up the whole kitchen.
He slammed the lid of the kettle shut,
and swore to be more careful.
His marriage couldn't afford another slip up.

# Poets & Poetry in Society

Who are they? Why are they so crucial? What type of person is one? It'll take a bit of digging to help you gain a clearer picture of who they are and how powerful a force they can be, as they are complex beasts, and together they hold society together as we know it. As for poetry—well, it's poems, isn't it, which come in all shapes and sizes, being used throughout human history, perhaps more than you realise.

Cast your mind back to Germany when the Nazis were running the show. They were a bloody awful lot and did so many things that we stood against and that's why we went at them to tell them off. It's a good job too because they were the kind of people that would have kept pushing their luck forever and ever. They were an *awful* lot. And so we ask ourselves the question, how did it go that far? There's a few reasons for it, but we're going to focus on one—language. Those bastards weaponised language to advance their cause and it was a key component of them being allowed to get more and more awful. To cut a long and awful story short, they very much dehumanised the Jews and made the transition into the Holocaust easier because of it. The only thing that would have made it worse for me is if they had used the Queen's English, but luckily, they used German.

Propaganda seeped into German folks' minds without them even knowing so, gradually turning a slightly cold but reasonably normal population into a group of awful people. A significant factor in why this worked so well and why they were seemingly unchallenged in their plans was—yep, you guessed it—the absence of poets. The antidote to propaganda is poetry. There weren't enough bloody poets because the slightly cold but reasonably normal German population didn't cultivate the observers, the romantics, the dreamers. No one was giving the German people a different language that made them second-guess what they'd been told by the awful Nazis. I have the utmost respect for those brave civilians who would house Jews and hide them under their rugs etc., but that was never going to be enough, was it? Which raises the most significant question of all— where were the fucking poets in all of this? They should have been scurrying around town, slipping tiny poems into people's pockets for them to discover when they got home and changing people's perspective on the world, building up a resistance to the awful Nazis day by day and eventually overthrowing them. Where were the fucking poets when we needed them most?

They would have saved all manner of bloodshed, and in the end, poets from England had to step in and sort the whole atrocity out. The sheer courage and will to self-sacrifice of the soldiers that crossed the sea on D-Day is well documented, which I make fair in my mind, but we're not told often enough about the other warriors at the *back* of the boats—the poets. These brave daydreamers would cast aside their internal squabbling about love, whether poems should have to rhyme and whether haikus are shit, to band together in the face of an awful evil, to protect all that they loved. Once the proper soldiers had cleared the beach of Germans, and danger of any kind, the brave poets would jump out of the boat to feel the sand between their toes. They'd written poems in the folds of paper aeroplanes and were floating them around France to influence enemy troops. If they had a particularly poignant poem, they'd strap it to an old grenade that wasn't explosive and toss it across enemy lines. Of course, in the end, the war was ended by a combination of standard military action *and* poetry, but it's reasonable to conclude, as you may have done already, that the legacy of those poems that the poets on our side were chucking at the enemy probably influenced the next generation enough to have prevented World War 3, without us even knowing there could have been one. A bullet to the brain is instant, but a poem lasts forever in the mind, or at least quite a while.

Now you know how God damn important poets are, you're probably wondering what type of character becomes one. Can it be taught or are they born with it? I tend to think it's the latter myself. Anyone can improve their language skills, but is a poem really about the technicalities of language? If poetry is about that, then the dictionary would be the best fucking poem of all time, and I can tell you that it isn't. No, a poet isn't a boffin, they are a creative force that makes you double take, perhaps by exposing a reality in your subconscious or transporting you to an imagined reality. A true poet sits just outside of society, but close enough to dip their toe in, so you are able to relate to them, whilst they are able to drag you away from the minute-by-minute bore of daily life.

And don't worry, you really don't have to enjoy award-winning poets' work or feel like you just don't get it when you should. I've seen some of the award-winning tripe swanning about the place nowadays and I can tell you as a poet, some of it really is tripe or, to coin a phrase I'll expand on later in the book, wet shite. You'll find plenty of imagery used to describe an emotion, or some smell that reminds them of a lover or a time in their childhood, and then they'll use odd punctuation or spacing, and there'll be nothing engaging about it yet you're the idiot for not getting it. Is that really the only poetry that should be winning awards? Are they really the only poets we have at our disposal in case Germany gets too big for its boots again? The answer to both is no, they're just the ones that take up the most space in the poetry world.

Truth be told, poetry is so many different things, and so are poets. The reason some award-winning poets win awards for wet shite is because there are people who love that type of thing, and good for them. It's just that these types have a hold on poetry and its popular perception. I don't think it's an aggressive hold, far from it, but it's a hold. These types gravitate towards studying it because they take it more seriously, so naturally if you follow that journey out on a large enough scale, they end up judging poetry and people start to see poetry as that little world. It isn't though. There is more.

The idea of wet shite being poetry itself plays a huge part in me scrunching up my face and cringing when I call myself a poet, and tossing around the idea of calling myself a 'writer'. Because of this,

I will continue to use the phrase wet shite because it makes me smile, but I do maintain a healthy respect for that type of poetry. It's just that I know that more people would enjoy poetry if they didn't perceive it all to be that way and they were exposed to more of the fun stuff. It's the job of poets like me to push more poetry out there that's engaging, imaginative, sometimes brash, uses quite a lot of swear words and ultimately, saves the world. All I'm saying is, if the Germans come for our freedom again, it wouldn't be a bad idea to have some poems with words like fuck, shit and c\*\*t in them to lob at the bastards.

# Fresh Out the Womb

His face was beautiful,
Though he looked concerned,
His shoulders were broad,
Though his skin soft,
His thighs were thick,
Though his hamstrings supple,
His dick was enormous,
Though its demeanour unthreatening.
She'd birthed *another* poet.

There are still some controversial breeding programmes of poets in remote locations across the globe, though they are slowly closing down. When they were designed, they were expected to produce an army of romantic easy-going long-haired poetic clones, but the reality was very different. Purebred poets were incredibly difficult to control and almost impossible to challenge, so in the end a decision was agreed across borders to release them back into society with the aim of diluting their genes to allow more manageable poets to spawn naturally. This has made a lot of us a lot more reasonable.

# "About Me" by the Powers That Be

Henry Mulligan currently has a presence both online and on land. He is fundamentally a funny-minded man but would like to consider himself a musician. His keyboard style has been described as "soon to begin learning it" and he names many types of music and some artists as influences. He has been known to keep his private life really *very* private, explaining during a conversation to someone that he refuses to do any media interviews because they've never had the decency to ask him for one. When close friends and family were questioned about what he is like behind closed doors, they all immediately smiled and made reference to his "brilliance", before twitching as they recollected his *horrendous* flaws. He is widely regarded as the greatest living person and the best thing that has ever happened.

"A brilliant bastard"

"A beautiful poison"

"okay"

# "About Me" by Me

Ah, the about me spiel. A brief window into my interior. A brief window into what I'm comfortable with you knowing about me, whilst attempting to appear somewhat vulnerable, endearing and humble. In some ways a challenge to keep your attention too, because you're probably not overly interested in getting to know me and are just here for the book in general, so I shall keep this short and sweet (you decide if I sound sweet). I won't say what the correct reaction from you should be, though a hearty laugh, smack of the table and arms flung high into the air followed by a shuddering applause is not unheard of.

I am a man of unnoticeable height, above average build, reasonable intellect and subpar self-esteem, but this I will say, I'm a fucking good poet. And I don't write away vague emotional daydreams on the back of a tissue I've been using to dry my unnecessary tears. My shit's funny, even cutting. And voluminous (always thought volumous was a word but I've been put in my place by the powers that be). It's worth adding as a final note that I despise calling myself a poet and I don't blame you if you shivered when I described myself as a fucking good one. To put you at ease, all I will say at this stage is that, in keeping with the remarks about tissues and tears above, there will be no wet shite in this book. You won't catch me staring at a scenic view describing how love feels and all that wet shite. I've not felt love in a fucking long time, and I don't plan to.

So come on, bloody well like me.

## The Humble Hypocrite

If other people had my talent,
they would have insufferable egos,
but I am my own worst critic,
and I am the very finest critic around.

I keep this one on a small piece of paper and slip it across the table when I'm sitting opposite another poet. Their face turns a medium grey because they can't deny it's a bit smart and they can't objectively call me a buffoon who's ruining poetry by having some long-overdue fun with it. They usually end up with their head in their hands, then look up, remove their hands, look back down at me, let out an annoyed sigh, and that's when I kick the floor like a matador, throw the finger guns at them and go "clever innit".

It gives me the most punchable grin.

# *Shockingly* Short Stories

There are shockingly short stories here and there on future pages of this book. They are most definitely on the short side for a story, though they are in fact the longest pieces of work in this book. Sure, there'll be novelists out in the wild sniggering at my idea of a long piece of work, and I, in response, challenge them to read any of these critters out using one breath and one breath alone. Taking a leap of faith that none of them spearfish underwater for hours at a time, I expect I'd see them coughing up blood trying to get to paragraph four as they collapse off of their mahogany chair. One thing is for sure though, it's a *hammer* blow reading one of these whales out loud to someone who doesn't like it. I end up red in the face, breathless, *empty*. One person's uncontrollable laughter is another person's sneer, it seems. On top of that, one person will say something's funny or moving or so clever with *such* hidden meaning and the next person will say it's not funny and it moves them only to be upset and minorly offended. I've had to conclude, therefore, that I can't trust *anybody*. I suspect this lesson is one learned by all who create at any level. At first it feels a little like a concussion, like your reality has been knocked askew, and over time it turns into a steely resilience. If someone doesn't like what you write, you just go "What have you written?", and if they are a writer of any sort, you just go "Different audiences mate", and if they're some sort of comedic poet more successful than you, you hang your head and question the point of it all.

I actually reckon these are alright though. What I've done as well is add a bit of wizarding spice to the pot and made them genuinely rhyme... If we're talking proper rhyming poetry then I'll stand up to anyone and back them as *half* decent at least. I mean, these fuckers go well over one page and they *keep* rhyming. That's almost insane.

One day I'd love to find the right music and tone of voice to perform them live, but I've got some work to do in regards to finding my voice and having the aerobic capacity to use it. The back-up plan is to read them slowly to build tension and do some eye acting. Anyway, I want you to be comfortable, so because of their length, I've fit them into appropriate chapters and stuck SSS in the top right-hand corner as a warning for your eyes. I am trusting you to read them however you wish.

# Nature 'n' Life

Nature weaves its roots around most things in my life and I like it. I suspect it quite likes me too. Of course from time to time I get caught in the rain when I'd rather not be, but more often than not nature makes me feel a bit better, so it *must* like me to treat me like that. You wouldn't keep making someone you don't like feel better, but you might occasionally rain down on someone you do. It all makes sense, doesn't it.

Summer's the classic. Lots of people bang on about summer. It's so refreshing to catch your reflection and realise you have a tiny tan. It's so lovely to not feel rushed to "get the day in" because the day takes bloody ages. It's so pleasing to smell freshly cut grass and a mysterious barbeque, sniffing it down and knocking on their door to ask if there's a sausage spare. But aside from that stuff, it can get unbearably hot and make it impossible to get anything done. If you're reading this in England, you'll know what I mean, and you'll know too about the bellends saying they love it when it's forty degrees. These people just don't care about getting anything done, or maybe they're just "different" and I should celebrate our differences, but it's a bit too different for me, and I hate them.

Autumn might be my favourite season. Yes the colours are oh so pretty but it also feels like a massive relief when it cools down a bit. The summer sun has its place but when the two-week heatwave hits I'm absolutely done with it. That's where autumn comes in. Bloody lifesaver. I usually slap a tree around this time and say "thanks, you…"

Winter is useful for saying "Sod it, I'm staying in and under a blanket" and that's quite nice. Also, the rain at the back end of autumn tends to create a lot of soggy leaves on the floor, and winter removes the mess a bit. Other than that, it's just, you know, ok. It's not as bad as the summer two-week heatwave but it's no autumn. The other thing to mention is that some cafes, pubs, offices, any inside places, find it appropriate to turn the heating up to near-summer-heatwave levels so you end up moving from freezing cold to boiling hot whenever you go anywhere. I've been known to throw the back of my hand to my forehead, say "for heaven's sake" and just flop to the floor when this all gets too much for me.

And then there's the start of spring, where you can start saying "Sod it, I'm clocking off" at 4 p.m. and wander around outside. It's a quite brilliant feeling and I find myself doing massive nose breaths when I'm out there. It fuels one of my favourite hobbies: wandering. Wandering is vastly different to walking. With walking, you have a purpose. It could be distance, a destination, a dog walk, but basically there's a point to it. With wandering, you're choosing to be lost. Obviously I can't be totally lost as I wander, as I do need to return home safely at some stage, so to that extent my wander isn't genuinely aimless. There's also a point to it, I guess, which is not to have a proper point, but I don't want to be one of those fiddly debating knobheads arguing the pedantics. The feeling, though, is bliss. I let my legs flop, I move slowly, I look at virtually *everything* and I give my brain free rein to do whatever it wants. It often tries to figure out the sky. Anyway, the rest of spring is alright, and I found I had enough poems loosely based on or within nature and no one dared stop me from making this a whole chapter.

# The Fresh Air Will Do You Good They Say      (SSS)

The fresh air will do you good they say,
It helps clear out your mind,
The womb of Mother Nature,
Wrapped around your human bind.

I've thrust aside my reservations,
Laced up my outside boots,
Left at the door my limitations,
Strode out amongst the roots.

It's nippier than first I thought,
The blue skies lured me in,
My faith in my attire,
Has exposed my fragile skin.

I'm battling the shivers,
As they want what's best for me,
Their wisdom must hold truth,
Even if it's hard to see.

The wind now blasts upon my face,
My tears and snot combine,
My purple fingers useless,
As my teeth now start to grind.

My beard is full of dribble,
All crusty from the cold,
I've lost all sense of humour,

My mood now harsh and bold.

My world now sad and limp,
I've lost sight of what's to gain,
My mind is now a prisoner,
Inside my frozen brain.

I've lost all trust in others,
I grow weaker in the breeze,
My mind obscured by anger,
For the ones that made me freeze.

# Winter's Awful Beauty

The winter paint,
The crisp soft white,
A cold kind of magic,
Its spell so bright.

The shared excitement,
Our pet's surprise,
Our whole world seen,
Through different eyes.

Well my eyes doth blink,
I see fuck all,
I've torn my groin,
To fight a fall.

My feet soaked through,
My bollocks tight,
With every step,
I'm filled with fright.

My errand's a risk,
My movements tactical,
All previous joy,
Seemingly impractical.

This one was inspired by a minor injury and a major grievance. It very much builds on my clear frustration with anything that's close to resembling extreme weather, and you'd do well to fold this one into your pocket for a rainy day in case an adrenaline junky starts mouthing off about how great it all is. You'll smirk when they tear their groin from their torso walking to their car.

## Garden Centre Trip

I was in charge of *only* the pot.
What about this rose? I asked.
It smells rosy enough to me, maybe we should get three?
Her eyes wilted.
Her walk turned to a trot, but I, was lumbered with the pot.
My steps forced, slow and strained,
I hauled my head skywards.
She was gone.

A devastation of a poem.

Just a quick warning with this one coming up. It's actually almost like a little bit cute 'n' that, and might well be considered an *actual* poem. You decide for yourself.

## The Impressive Little Crow

I walked idly around my village,
My attention all but dead,
When I spotted a crow not flying,
He'd chosen to walk instead.

Then a magpie swooped towards him,
And offered a shiny thing,
The industrious crow said "keep it",
As he wasn't one for bling.

Then a squirrel scurried over,
And offered him a nut,
He said unless he found it himself,
His beak would remain shut.

Then a lady crow approached,
And offered him a dance,
He said "If you're that damn easy,
You haven't got a chance."

He knew life had no meaning,

Without hardship and a fall,
When in the air he wouldn't flap,
He'd grab the air and crawl.

He knew of the need for suffering,
So wise and in the know,
But how on earth had he figured it out?
The impressive little crow.

## Mental Wind

The wind was fucking mental.
It took ten minutes to get my car door open so I could get to the gym.
Had to get a limb inside, take the bruise as the door slammed me, then wriggle the rest in.
Unfortunately once there, I couldn't get *out* of the fucking door.
Being inside the car pushing outwards meant I didn't have access to my pulling muscles.
I ploughed on for a quarter of an hour before resigning to the fact I'd have to turn the power steering off for a workout.
I'm working from my phone now until the weather turns in my favour.

A really bad day all round here but the wind wasn't the worst thing demonstrated in this solid poem. It's the fact that you can work from your phone now. *Eww.* If you're not taking advantage of this remote miracle by sipping on an orange squash in Bora Bora, all it means is that work has their hands around your throat wherever you are. Try turning your notifications off in case that helps, but if you're anything like me you'll check stuff even more in case there are things you're not being notified about. This can extend gym sessions by double, ruin TV time and bugger up your sleep. Just delete it all from your phone and remain firm if questioned about your position on it. Your personal phone is for personal stuff, *alright.*

Some decent words thrown into this one. A point for each one you spot.

## Autumn Leaf

For a time or two,
My life has light,
Me and the gang,
Share colours bright.

The rain then starts to pour,
The sky morphs to grey,
I watch my friends all fall,
Each and every day.

Mud starts to squelch us all together,
As I too find myself on the floor,
Passers-by look down and frown,
And my life now feels quite poor.

The walkers see me as a nuisance,
My entire world has turned foggy,
They say that "moist" is the most repulsive word,
But they have never been called soggy.

## Hot Day

The day,
Extremely hot,
So I hopped into a cold shower,
And washed the day off,
Then stamped on it,
Told it to fuck off down the plug hole,
And off it did fuck.

I was melting but could somewhat see the funny side.

## Another Hot Day

Temp can't be denied,
My clothes I haven't tried,
I went outside and cried,
Put an egg on my leg, it fried,
Happiness, I scoff,
I'm in the devil's trough,
So hot that my eyes cough,
I wish the weather would sod off.

I'd forgotten what the funny side was by now.

This is a bit of a silly bugger but it might get you thinking a bit more than you usually do as you waltz about town or around the village, and the self-exploration might not be that comfortable for you. If it gets too much, I can gift you my strength. There's a small mention of pulling a groin again also. I tried to think of a different body part but the barebones of it all is that groins do tend to be one of the first things that go if you're not getting your walking spot on. That's just life.

## I'm Still Not Sure How to Walk

Left foot right foot,
Alternate the two,
This bit's well embedded,
The rest's a bit askew.

When I think about my arms,
The swing becomes quite gentle,
When I fall back into autopilot,
They go fucking mental.

I'm not sure of my stride,
I try a shuffle to remove some length,
I try a long one but pull my groin,
As my legs don't have the strength.

What the fuck is going on with my feet?

I close my eyes and let one dangle,
Then let it drop down on the ground,
And hope to find the correct angle.

I'm shuffling striding and swinging,
With my eyes closed like a muppet,
Who the hell is in charge of this mess?
Am I a fucking puppet?

The more I bloody think,
The less I walk like me,
I've changed technique so many times,
I've walked into a tree.

## Winter Bin Feet

It was colder than his imagination,
And the bins further than his memory,
Meaning his house slippers weren't enough,
Weren't enough to stop his feet from freezing,
So he shuffled back in a bit panicky,
To pop his feet in the oven,
Whack 'em on a low heat.

This falls into the category of "ok if you're sure this is ok to be published". I've scattered them around the book so they're spaced out and don't make you question me.

## Bed Bug

When you meet a bed bug,
Don't squish,
Instead,
Say hi,
Let's get you out of bed,
Would you like to see the lounge?

My cute side. Don't tell a soul.

This one could have been housed in the "About the House" chapter but I thought the extremity of winter stood slightly taller than the love and appreciation of carpet (poet's talk).


## Wishful Winter Carpet

The conditions were at their very coldest,
And the same pains cast upon me each day,
From the quite serious storms,
To the wincing first step out of bed in the morning,
Where my feet try to tense their way up into my shin,
Before they touch the ice-cold hardwood floor,
And are literally gagging for carpet.

End strong. That's what they say, all over the planet, so I've done some rhyming for the end of this chapter. Think of it as fireworks for poetry.

## Peaceful Morning Lap

I want to take my dog outside,
My lovely little boy,
A quiet lap before the day,
I hope it gives us joy.

The beauty in the primitive,
The calm it puts in you,
Taking your little companion,
For a simple wee and poo.

I'm greeted by the postman,
A different one each day,
I've thrown them a "good morning",
What else have I to say?

The neighbour's popped their head out,
I can see their little smirk,
Again I have to greet them,
It's feeling more like work.

A few yards further forward,

I'm barely out my flat,
Here comes Captain Knobhead,
Another loud-mouthed prat.

I can't quite stomach this,
I've barely got a friend,
Yet on this tiny morning lap,
The socials never end.

I've one more chance for peace,
If the park feels all majestic,
But the geese have other plans,
They're having a domestic.

roar!

# Work

It's horrendous isn't it. *Really*. There's probably some easy-going twats out there that don't mind it, some purpose-led wallies that find real, genuine meaning in their work. But for the rest of us, it very rarely feels like anything other than an excruciating slog. A slog littered with mind-numbing tasks, bothersome key performance metrics and other humans making it all harder (that's a big one). It'll play odd tricks on you too, making you develop a new mindset every other week just to try and cope with the damn thing. I even came up with a bloody mantra once. I thought to myself that "If you accept how little you can do, you'll be surprised by how much you do." It's a cock's way of saying one thing at a time, one day at a time etc. I find it hard to believe that I'd have spoken to myself quite so much like a cock if it wasn't for work.

There *was* a time when I really appreciated the friends that I would have at work, but after moving around a few times you can't help but accept that you'll forget about each other when one of you moves on. It's got to the stage, to be frank, that I start cutting them loose in my mind when they pay more attention to their work than they do to my boredom-fueled, borderline pestlike desire to chat to them. It's just fucking rude if you ask me.

Through all this, I've learned there are two things you need to do to survive at work. If you've got a personality, you need to batter that thing down so it can't rise to the surface, and you need to "manage up". "Manage up" in plain English means "brown nose the life out of people and replace any moans you want to let out with solutions or questions that deflect away from how you feel" (batter those feelings down good and proper). You could add a third must-do if you need reminding of it, but it's more than likely something you do anyway, and that's pretending to care. Very few of us manage to find the courage to turn around to a superior at work and say "Do you know what, I literally couldn't care less, this is meaningless to me." I've always had a little urge to go off on one explaining how much more they have invested in the job, be it through a higher salary or a stake in the business so they can profit from shares. The flip side to that line of thinking is that you fight hard and work your way up, but with how wages stack up against life costs for my generation, my thinking steers towards telling them to fuck off because it's not worth the stress.

To be fair though, if you're one of my good-humoured, mature, highbrow readers, you're probably one of those twats climbing the workplace ladder at a sensible and sustainable pace, gradually increasing your financial standing in the world and building a solid LinkedIn presence. If you're not doing that, you must be one of my odd, problematic misfits, and I love you all the *more* for it.

# The Office Hello

She wandered in from a different designated office space,
With not a care in the world,
She slapped her notebook down on my desk,
"Hi, I haven't met you yet! Do you always sit here or do you all
move around?"
My face started smothering how it felt,
"It changes," I explained,
My eyes moved from her to her notebook,
It wasn't supposed to be there,
"Any notes in there for me?"
"Ooh that'd be telling wouldn't it!"
I digested the concept,
"Ok, I'll make a note of it,"
My joke flew past this social hurricane,
I was exhausted,
I did a crack-worthy close of my laptop,
Like an angry Pac-Man,
And paced to the kitchen,
"I think I need a coffee!"
And apparently so did she,
As she followed me,
No doubt to tell me about where she parked and how long she'd
worked here,
But I had nothing left for her,
I'd left my get up and go on my ergonomic chair,
I was just slumped movements and generic words.

If this poem doesn't register with you then you are far, far too popular and outgoing to be reading this book and I demand you slap it shut immediately. Shoo! Go! Go on… Scram!

## Too Tired

My decisions were making themselves,
My eyes worked but I was blind,
My tongue worked but it was huge,
My throat was angry at me,
My skull had shrunken to tell me off,
I was too tired for this shit.

Now in case any of you are not aware, a WeWork is just a shared office space. Chancers and free spirits from all sorts of companies go there to get away from being stuck in their own home. To get away from being at home but feeling trapped by work still. *Eww*. It's very much like the watering hole of modern work, and like all watering holes out in the actual wild, experiences differ in regards to hydration and danger.

## WeWork – Bank

It was an adult nursery,
People playing grown-ups but it was an illusion,
It was a cesspit of dishonest actors,
Each floor climbed strengthening the hot stench of modern working,
Stern folk keeping focus on their laptop screen and trying to forget they're sitting next to strangers,
Guests and colleagues in the lobby greeted with cold enthusiasm,
Rah-rah big business types shaking each other down with a scoffing great smile,
Couple of el chapos with small woolly hats playing pool and exhausting the phrase "short form content",
But none of us *actually* liked each other,
And if our MacBook 3000's weren't company property,
We'd have been throwing our toys at each other's heads.

## Terrorist Catcher

I wasn't very good at fishing,
So I became a CIA agent,
And I caught terrorists instead,
I'd hang a rod out the chopper,
With an evil plan at the end of it,
And reel the bastards in one after the other,
My favourite part was seeing them all scrambling around in the net,
They looked ridiculous.

Contact my publisher should you need my help with this sort of thing, and use the subject line "terrorist bastards: need Henry".

## Work Zoom

Rookie error,
As a non-stakeholder,
A mute participant,
Allowing all attendees into my lounge,
But the camera was on now,
My introduction as a nobody done,
My body out of sorts,
Where to put my hands,
Where to put my eyes,
I kept my hands stiff as hell on the arms of my chair,
My naive eyes glanced downwards at my phone,
Which was not professional and not ok,
So I moved them,
To every corner of the room,
Which didn't look normal,
Which looked like a shit slow robot tracking a fly,
I had to stop drawing a big square with my eyes,
Move them to roughly the centre of the screen,
I couldn't remember if blinking was permitted,
How long was left on this call?
I was a prisoner in my own screen.

I actually received the approval of a friend's older brother for this analysis so if it's not to your taste, maybe you should take it up with him. I'm also not *totally* convinced calls like this weren't initially trialled in Guantanamo but I'd like to flesh out my theory for a couple of years further before I jump on any podcast with a couple of cowboys from the conspiracy community. I don't want to look like a fool.

## Tired of It

It was the sixth question from her manager that day,
It was the fourteenth reason she was trying as to why it was all worth it,
She was growing tired of reason.

Notes for modern fierce female readers: Poor you (with respect).

Notes for old-fashioned readers: Poor cow.

## Sales Discovery Call

Another prospect was booked in for a right discovering.

I couldn't be arsed.

My hand drew my phone closer to my head and my head leaned away but it could never outrun my hand.

The prospect picked up and we threw around some standard niceties and fake laughter.

I moved things on to business and tore a question clean out of the sales best practice handbook.

The prospect answered "Just talk normally please" and fucked me right over.

I tore another one out of the book, something like "Would a solution for this benefit your workload?" or some shite similar.

They said "Solutions, by definition, always fucking help don't they."

I was panicking and went to ask for referrals but didn't mention the context so just said "Do you know anyone?"

The whole thing was recorded on our system.

## Work Christmas Social

We had a few options on the table,
So many that bowling didn't get a whiff,
Nor axe throwing,
A hotly contested poll was undertaken,
And Topgolf grabbed pole position,
With the escape room a close second,
I took it upon myself to email Topgolf,
I asked if they could remove all the exit signs when we came,
Lock all the doors,
Escape golf...

I actually didn't go to this in the end and it wasn't because Topgolf denied my requests via not responding to them at all. It was because we headed into the dreary office that looked like it'd been pulled straight out of Microsoft Windows 95 for an hour-long department meeting at 3.30-ish, and we were told beforehand by the director that we'd head off to have some fun after the meeting. Sounds great, right? Well it wasn't. This disappointing director of a man said after the meeting concluded that we'd head off about six, half six, up to two hours after the meeting, to which my eyes replied *are you fucking kidding me*, and my clenched fists yelled *you slime*. I couldn't make it because my dog-sitting arrangements didn't align well and it's a perfect example of how some workplaces expect you to hang your entire life up and put it back on when it suits *them*. Well I've got two things to say to this slime now. Number one: I never meant to get your dog's name wrong but I know it wound you up, so if I see you again I'm going to use the wrong name on purpose and call it a cat. Number two: fuck you, I've got a book.

## Late to Work

I was late to work,
because the best barbers in town had cancellations,
so I managed to book some last minute haircuts,
for my moles.

## Sales Training Call

Fucking sales training call.
Sweat fest.
I'd been bashing through 'em on my own doing anything I could to
get my call times up.
I was bending rules but to my credit, still bashing.
Now my manager stands over me like a fucking vulture over a
carcass.
A nervous carcass.
I'm saying any and all of the words I can remember into the phone.
He's staring at my sweat.
I've twisted so my body leans on the side of my thigh, squashing
and concealing my phone.
He couldn't know could he?
That I'm on the phone to my own mobile...
*Fuck.*

## Hitcoin – Invest Now!

My new business idea,
Hitcoin,
Which is Bitcoin but better,
Each Hitcoin is worth more than a Bitcoin,
Each Hitcoin is shinier than a Bitcoin,
The whole currency of Hitcoin is much more stable,
It is immune to volatility,
And if any new investors are wondering about timescales,
Strategy etc.,
It will only take roughly a year to dominate the market,
As we will use marketing,
Including the utilisation of billboards,
And putting some messages on interweb forums,
On top of always calling Bitcoin Shitcoin,
So that's success year one,
And when we are the biggest colour in the market pie chart,
We will start to commandeer other pie charts,
Until we are the only colour everywhere.

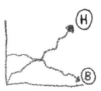

Contact my publisher if interested in investing. Minimum £10,000 investment. Terms and Conditions will be used against you.

Here comes another "ok if you're sure this is ok to be published". I look across the table at them and go "I know you'll say you're just a mere publisher and I am, in fairness largely because of you, a semi-professional poet so I know what's best, but are you *sure* this one should be published. I mean have you *really* looked at it, looked through it. Are you *sure*?"

## Subway – Look Fresh

Women were only eating avocados,
And men didn't want sandwiches anymore,
They wanted their penises to look nicer,
So Subway changed their signs and became a chain of pejazzle stations,
Knobway,
Decorating across the nation,
Especially handy in the mini Subways within petrol stations when you were on the move,
Even more so if on the way to a date,
"Footlong or 6-inch sir?"
"Come on mate, don't wind me up."
"It's a 6-inch hearty Italian."
"I know it's not a wholemeal."
I asked for my initials in dried sweetcorn,
And to tuck a bit of turkey in the foreskin to make a meat scarf,
Topped off with a risky sweet onion sauce,
I was worried it might make her cry.

# Mental Health (ish)

I think I hear these two words more often than I hear "good morning", and I'm torn on the whole thing. I can't say it's a bad thing for the topic to be more accepted as something to talk about, heavens no, but sometimes I turn into an ever-so-slightly grumpy oik about the topic. Sometimes it feels to me like the people talking most are relatively stable people going through unstable patches of life. These can be harrowing of course and being open about them *is* a fantastic thing as it allows people to get help in whatever form best suits them, so I'm definitely not saying it's a bad thing overall. In fact, I think it's probably a significant net positive overall. Significant enough to ignore the people who just turn to moaning and actually require a bit of backbone really. It's just that a lot of this stuff is acute. I worry about anyone with *chronic* diagnosable challenges, needing lifelong management. You're not going to deep breathe your way out of being autistic are you (?).

The phrase "Neuro-familiarity breeds contempt" can easily be extended with a little bit of creative licence to many of these chronic conditions. The idea is that neurotypical people (the norms) can relate to many of the symptoms neurodivergent (the abnorms?) people experience but because they're able to manage them, contempt is bred towards the abnorms because why can't they just manage them better? It's akin to you saying to someone with narcolepsy who keeps falling asleep at the wheel, "Totally get it, I sleep too, but I wouldn't sleep in the car if I was you." Or you might have a great day followed by a *shocker* but it doesn't mean you're bipolar. You get the gist. This type of shit is also hardly ever included in the heartwarming progressive initiatives and training courses you are subjected to in modern workplaces that care more about what colour your skin is or where you stick your knob (I'd say or fanny but you can't really stick a fanny anywhere, I don't think—at least not the ones I've met).

I'm probably just being grumpy because I'm one of the abnorms who doesn't have the headspace to care for some of that stuff. I've got to create a life that adapts to me as best I can, because I can't adapt that well to life. Mind you, if people were always mentioning my conditions in a super understanding way, I'd be liable to last a week before I said "I'm not a label!", and sometimes I think some ancient wisdom from philosophers that have long been turned into marble for tourists' eyes would be enough for basically anyone to get by. You just can't win with me. I can't tell you what disorders I have (I'm explaining why shortly), but I wonder if perhaps I've got some sort of nightmare disorder, and *I'm* the fucking nightmare. Speak to someone if you're feeling shit though, whoever the hell you are. Chances are if you're reading this book, you've got a bit of mental in you.

*I* have two *unnamed* "disorders". My psychiatrist has blurted out their names on a number of occasions but every time he does I slip my hand under his notepad, slap it upwards so it whacks him in the chops, take his pen, press it against his lips and go "ssh, it's for your notes, not mine." Having them unnamed in my own mind creates a bit of mystery around the whole thing. Similar to how feeling the presence of someone who has passed away would be ruined if someone qualified in that sort of thing said "They're over there", and it turns out they're not saying anything supportive as a guiding presence, they're just doing all the things that pissed you off when they were living. The *mystery* is the special feeling. What have I got? Are either of them one of the good ones? Are either of them one of the bad ones? Who am I a danger to? Me? Others? Both? I can lose myself in thoughts about the mystery for days on end. Maybe there's one called Mystery Disorder and I'm lost in that, but something tells me that wasn't what came out of my psychiatrist's bruised mouth.

Having two disorders which could literally be anything to my knowledge makes it a lot easier to connect with people who know what they've got. I listen to what they're going through and reply with "Yep, you're preaching to the choir, I've got it too." I'm not lying because I don't know that I don't. I'm *relating* to people, and getting five to six free dinners a month from all the support groups I keep getting invited to. You don't have to be crazy to get an invite, but it helps (they *roar* when I say this). Most people there are obviously pretty darn neurotic so the snacks are important to help keep everyone occupied and away from their thoughts. Say what you want about mentals, they put on a fucking amazing spread.

I don't *really* have anything jaw-dropping to say on mental health, I just have some poems that needed a home created for them and therefore had to spew out an introduction with very *very* incoherent thoughts about the whole thing. I think you'll get through them and find something that grabs your eye in one or two, to make you feel at home. Chances are if you've read the constructed nonsense in the last few paragraphs and you're *still* reading, you've probably actually got quite a lot of mental in you, so you'll feel *very* at home.

# My Therapist Is a Twat

I visited my therapist,
I felt completely beat,
They told me to stand in the corner,
I wasn't allowed a seat.

I explained a tricky problem,
I started to share my trauma,
They asked if the problem was mine or theirs,
Then confirmed it was the former.

I hunched my way a bit closer,
I presented a stress-ridden frown,
They suggested I push past my breaking point,
Until I reach breakdown.

I shed a pathetically slow tear,
I crumpled to my knees,
They informed me my existence was
beyond anyone's expertise.

I stuttered a couple of words,
I noticed their face freeze,
They said my pain was the first reported case,
Of a mental infectious disease.

I was desperate for some help,
I thought of Freud and enquired,
They claimed if he'd have studied me,

From psychology he'd have retired.

Sigh.

## Therapy Defence

She headed to therapy,
Walked stiffly through the door,
Went eye to eye with the damn shrink,
Threw a quick head nod,
Kept marching,
Sat down fast,
Put her shades on,
Then her earmuffs,
She was having none of it,
No one was getting in her head today.

## Nice Thought of the Day

No matter how bad today gets,
just know,
there is someone out there,
having a fucking nightmare,
using thin tin foil.

# I Disagreed with My Sectioning (SSS)

I shouldn't have been sectioned, what had you been smoking?
When I heard the news, I thought you must be fucking joking,
I only did one poo in public, and now I'm all locked up,
Just you see how I behave in here, I'll make you feel a schmuck.

Met the man with multiple personalities,
A different one each time,
Trying to change their ways,
I told them they were fine.

There's a man with OCD,
Obsessed with the number three,
I turn the volume up to four,
When he's watching TV.

The anorexic is fucking terrified,
Of what the chef is cooking,
I put extra on her plate,
Whenever she's not looking.

I cuddle up to the bipolar,
She's manic and wants a dare,
I challenge her to take her meds,
And she goes fucking spare.

There's a boy with extreme ADHD,
He fucking hates sitting still,
So I use my extra bodyweight,

And sit on him against his will.

Someone else has got Tourette's,
Has a swear jar to keep calm,
Any time I want some cash,
I go and pinch their arm.

Self-harmer in the corner,
Maybe I should warn her,
The razor blades are rubber,
But I'm happy to club her.

The murderer's getting bored,
His urge has been ignored,
I sit him next to a nervous man,
Claim he just slagged off his Nan.

Like clockwork the staff jump in,
Lanyards round their neck,
I snatch one off a slow one,
And they all shout flipping heck.

I shouldn't be locked up,
It's giving me anxiety,
I'm only mad in here,
Not out there in society.

Your decorating is suffocating,
It encourages demise,
I only scratch the walls,

So that there's something for my eyes.

If you don't get me out of here,
I'm ready to attack,
When I next meet the shrink,
I'll start diagnosing back.

I shouldn't be in here,
No maybes ifs or buts,
Any sane person thrown in here,
Would be driven fucking nuts.

# The New Psychopaths

Psychopaths weren't as exciting anymore.
The days of bloodcurdling shenanigans had dwindled,
confined to half-dark documentaries,
or binge-worthy boxsets,
observed with snack-filled platters,
as the blood of the innocent splatters.
The new psychopaths had no edge.
They would post PowerPoint-esque slides of borderline loony
political opinions,
create extremists out of the ordinary,
find bravery in the safest of spaces,
regurgitate anything that sounded half moral,
whilst kindly sharing tiny clips of the live music gig for us to listen to,
inspiring our takeaway faults with a picture of theirs,
and ensuring we have a picture of their positive covid test as soon
as their eyes see it.
It was death by a thousand sighs,
rather than bludgeoning,
or a machete to the neck.
The new psychopaths were pathetic.


Bloody technology again, innit. Makes us stupiderer. I'm not political and I hope to God I never turn out to be. I've seen too many bandwagons jumped on and too many good friends breaking their spines falling off them when it turns out to be a load of tosh. I'm not better than them, I just use up too much brainpower consciously trying to think critically that I never end up with enough time to actually form an opinion on anything.

## My Eyes Need Boundaries

My eyes needed boundaries,
They were looking at everything,
People with glasses,
Lady's arses,
Attractive men without an explanation,
My eyes weren't designed for such freedom,
My eyes needed boundaries,
We agreed acceptable targets,
They could watch cars,
They could watch wildlife,
They could watch the wind,
And anything outside of that would result in a lashing,
I would lash my own eyes,
For my eyes aren't built to yield unchallenged power,
My eyes need boundaries.

If you ever find your eyes are getting a bit cheeky for your liking/ their own good, check if they took their cheeky monkey tablets that morning!!!

# I Can't Even Be Trusted to Kill Myself      (SSS)

Life has really got to me,
Every day is shitty,
But ending it takes skill and craft,
I might stick with self-pity.

The sulk is rather rotten,
All I do is wallow,
I've got forty-eight paracetamol,
But my throat's too sore to swallow.

I've got a ceiling fan above,
And a rope that's really soft,
But I'm no good with knots,
And the ladder's in the loft.

I see the crack den isn't far,
They've an overdose platoon,
But my clothes have just been washed,
And I haven't got a spoon.

The local bridge is calling,
I don't do things by halves,
But to hop up on the sides,
I would likely strain my calves.

Besides I've got no friends,
To lend a hand and push,
And I can't do it on my own,

I'm scared of being mush.

I could stand out on the road,
Get smothered by a truck,
But I cannot trust my instincts,
To not dodge and dive and duck.

The sharp knife's in the drawer,
My path to wrists is clear,
But if I went to slit the things,
My aim would not get near.

I could run myself a bath,
And lie in it face down,
But to be found in that position,
I'd feel too much of a clown.

A fork in a plug socket,
It would be rather drastic,
But it wouldn't work for me,
My cutlery is plastic.

The roof jump's still an option,
Whilst my life doesn't matter,
But I'd land on something soft,
I'm incapable of splatter.

There's that hard bloke down the pub,
I could punch him in the face,
But he wouldn't even bother,

He'd just call me a disgrace.

If I head down to the station,
To be clattered by a train,
They'd rather swerve right off the tracks,
Than touch my life's disdain.

Fast food could be the answer,
Exploding innards may be best,
But my legacy might read terrorist,
With the internal suicide vest.

I'll just burst like a balloon,
With a knot tied in my willy,
So my legacy will simply read,
*Dangerously* silly.

The interesting thing with that one is that our loyal contemporary, silliness, didn't come across very well when I posted it on Instagram. I thought it was obvious but seven people contacted me asking if I was ok. Half of me thought it was nice and half of me thought people just didn't know me very well, which, if anything, pushed me closer to actually being depressed. I believed it to be over before I received a call from the police saying someone had reported me as a danger to myself (for real). They arrived at my house and I had to show them I was fine. *Imagine* me being dragged into a police car against my will screaming "*Please believe me!*" and "*I've never felt better!*" Thank you to whoever reported me as my own worst enemy.

## Bereft of Hope

He was bereft of hope,
questioning the point,
the point of his active efforts to be more organised,
as the cashier started to scan his shopping in total random order,
virtually laughing at the neat piles he had made,
acting like a grabby octopus on a wind up.
His psychologist had warned this sort of thing could happen.

## A Sulk of a Day

The day was a disaster,
He felt well sulky,
Everything and nothing was his fault,
He couldn't win,
He went for a walk with his top off,
Just wanted the midges to suck his blood,
But it was December,
Why had no one told him,
He berated some foxes in retaliation,
Told 'em they are a poor man's dog,
None of the discipline,
Charlatans,
They moved on,
He was still pissed through with pity,
A neighbour observed with their notepad,
"Possible nonce."

This is a firm favourite of many friends. We've all emailed the government to get it onto the syllabus.

## The Sequel Sulk

The previous day lingered,
Plus he'd been penned as a potential paedo,
So there was that,
He went for a walk with his top on,
Smiled respectfully at others,
Stayed well away from wildlife,
Punished himself in subtler ways,
Stepping in every puddle,
Feet all squelchy and disgusting,
Hitting the jackpot with a deep mud puddle,
Browning him to his knees,
He looked ridiculous,
But he didn't really realise,
And was still beaming his smile at everyone,
He'd actually made things worse somehow,
Neighbours up to five doors down,
Ushering their children inside.

## The Loneliest Man in the World

He was the loneliest man in the world,
As he singlehandedly,
Tried to double bag a bin bag.

I think I fucked up a bit here. I might have moved past devastating and become harrowing.

## I Am Trying to Be Mindful

I am trying to be mindful,
So I can be a bit more brave,
As currently to my existence,
I am nothing but a slave.

I've sat and crossed my legs,
Taken my socks off too,
There'll be no internal rumblings,
As I've just been to the loo.

I'm inhaling through my nose,
I've snorted too much in,
I've exhaled in a panic,
So it doesn't burst my skin.

I'm observing through my body,
I'm starting with my toes,
I'll move up extra slowly,
Let's see how this goes.

My feet are feeling tingly,
Like they are stuck in mud,
My crossed legs crushing down on them,
They're struggling for blood.

I cannot feel my shins at all,
But I know that they are there,
My knees feel extra knobbly,

Now I'm not sitting on a chair.

My thighs feel tight for space,
My groin is hard to find,
My hips and lower back are sore,
From the relentless daily grind.

I don't know what my mid-back is,
So I'm going straight up top,
My traps need a good old spa day,
How long till I can stop?

My neck is feeling tired,
Supporting my big old head,
I wore a vest in the garden yesterday,
So my shoulders just feel red.

I'm travelling down my arms,
My elbows are cracking up,
My hands are being wriggly,
They simply won't let up.

It might be the breeze from the window,
Or feeling full from all my snacks,
But I'm starting to get the hang of this,
I'm starting to relax.

I'm taking another breath,
And exhaling all my trouble,
Any thought that's floating in,

I'm bursting like a bubble.

All the work has now been done,
I've completely emptied my head,
Except for one nagging question,
Am I mindful, or am I dead?

## Dear Parents

Am I you?
Or am I you?
Are some bits you?
Other bits you?
Who the bleeding hell am I?
I know nothing of you,
You know nothing of me,
You know more of you,
I know more of me,
But I know that in my darkest moments,
I am the very worst of both of you,
And in my very finest hours,
I am entirely self-made.

## New Teeth

I had veneers put in,
and I looked fantastic,
but I hated myself.
My self-esteem had somehow *dropped*.

## The Ha(r)sh Brownie

He was the only one in the group who'd never been to this kind of
coffee shop.
The teasing was borderline excessive by this point.
He ordered a harsh brownie by mistake,
It was a *damningly* bitter pill to swallow.

## Gap Year

I wanted to find myself,
and I did,
but I didn't like me,
so I put myself back.

# Things You Wish You Could Ignore

The loo roll's last sheet,
The dieting urge to cheat,
The hole in the sock,
The size of your cock,
The yellow armpit stain,
The early alarm for your train,
The hard squeeze for the toothpaste,
The healthy dinner's real taste,
The loud grunter at the gym,
The urge to punch him,
The rejection from a lover,
The unwashed bed cover,
The man against you on the tube,
The squelch of his sweaty boob,
The wave from the neighbourly fellow,
The police officer's hello,
The disappointing coffee,
The belly ache from toffee,
The slightly long toenail,
The skin that's oh so pale,
The wage against the cost,
The dreams that you have lost,
The inner demon killer,
The face that's in the mirror,
The opposite opinion,
The customer service minion,
The number on the scales,
The work colleague's tales,

The ignorance of youth,
The sudden unhealthy tooth,
The amount of time you've wasted,
The heartache you've tasted,
The number of real friends,
The night-out evening ends,
The loved ones that have gone,
The email that's a con,
The positives of a hard day's work,
The responsibilities that you can't shirk,
The piling up of dirty clothes,
The accidental lunchtime doze,
The shoulder that's gone stiff,
The daydream off a cliff.

I miss the days before 'em,
As a kid who never saw 'em,
Never will I adore 'em,
But it's best I don't ignore 'em.

# Love (The Swine)

There are lots of different types of love and *all* carry significance. There are very few who would deny, however, that whilst tragedy can be equally as intense across the different forms, humour tends to pop up more often with the romantic kind. I mean you *can* find moments of humour joking about a dead relative, but those moments just seem to crop up less often than in the world of romantic love. I'd say it'd take at least twice as long on average to joke around about a dead relative than it would to joke around about someone ripping your heart out and shitting on it. For myself I'd say the lines are more blurred, but I'm going on about averages. I'm trying to use stats, that I've guessed.

I do wonder if dating has gone down the shitter in modern times. I'm not saying that the sexual revolution in the sixties was a mistake, because I couldn't really explain what it was, but it's worth at least *drafting* an opinion that it might have been a bad egg dressed as a pudding. Pretty much everyone seems a bit flaky in these times, as if shopping around is the safest bet to find someone compatible. And that logic isn't the worst logic I've heard this week, that's for sure. It just feels like basically no one bothers to try, and if you do you're going to freak people out. The emotionally stable among us, along with the mellower personalities, probably navigate this space with reasonable ease. It's the odd, problematic misfits with more intense personalities that require a little more time to get to know...

I can't say I've been a perfect example of a well-intentioned, patient potential lover. There is that also. A girl on a dating app once told me she doesn't like dairy and I replied "That's funny because you look like a right cow." To my credit, she laughed and I'd judged the atmosphere correctly, but I'm pretty sure I'm not married to her so perhaps comments like that should be put through a reviewal process in future.

Technology has really buggered shit up too. That might indeed be the biggest thorn in our side. Next to no one is on a dating app to ramp up their search for a significant other. The apps just lie dormant on our phones, like little diet social media platforms that you turn to when you're having a poo. We're too used to them being there, to having all these people in our pockets. Wind back to a time before the app store and you didn't have thousands of people in your pocket. You couldn't be blasé about getting to know someone if you got their number because you knew it could be at a minimum a few months before someone else gave you the chance. If I got a girl's number in 2011, I was *really* getting to fucking know her.

A couple of weekends ago (as I write this) I commandeered a number from a young woman in a bar. My friend made the introductions when I was in the loo so I only had to return from my piss, say hello, grip my fleece in my hand for dear life and get enough words out to let the awkwardness subside over the course of the first five minutes. Fast forward an hour and a half and she's flirting like a monster and giving me her number. We genuinely got on and she showed all the right signs. Fast forward a further 24 hours and I'm staring at her face on WhatsApp saying "Why, Penny, *why* won't you reply?" It was a kick to the confidence. I eventually managed to see the funny side of her forgetting I'm alive and sent her a picture of myself at the British Science Museum in front of a model train that'd been taken earlier in the day saying "You could have had this", followed by one of me laughing as I walked through British Science Museum saying "Now I'm walking away". I sent a couple more texts over the next two days that I thought were funny, but after the reaction from friends being split 50:50 between hilarious and creepy, I left her alone to wallow in my memory. And here's the point on what the problem is. I'm the weird one here for making a joke out of it and "being weird". I'm the weird one for being confused that someone could be *so* devious. But really take a look at this for a second. Talking to someone for an hour and a half, flirting with them, connecting with them, willingly giving your phone number to them so you could keep talking and arrange a date, to then just ignore them completely... that's fucking sociopathic, and we've been conditioned to think it's weirder to be jarred *by* sociopathic behaviour than to be guilty *of* the damn thing itself. It's the work of swines. So if you're reading this Penny, you fucking sociopath, I've moved on. It's just a shame your name hasn't from the 1930s.

# I Can Read My Girlfriend's Mind

I can read my girlfriend's mind,

I'm quite good at it but I hate what's in there so I lose my nerve,

I just kind of duck and dive until I find the neck and work my way

down until I fall out her arsehole.

# The Woman and the Poo

The classically sexy blond hair wandered into the carriage,

Ripping my eyelids open and penetrating my world,

My brain was full of oohs and phwoars and oh my god I love yous,

She didn't peer over at me which was fine,

It meant I couldn't get a sly stare at her eyes and so a bit of mystery remained for moi,

She sat a yard from me,

A million miles away,

My earphones couldn't match my yearning for her phone conversation,

My ears standing to attention upon hearing which pub she's going to,

A pub I knew,

A pub I could chitter chatter about,

She was tossing around the idea of just changing tops rather than dressing up,

For the notoriously pretentious pub,

Something I could use to bond our minds as I myself sat slumped in a tee shirt,

But alas the next train stop was reality,

As I peered down at my fleece scattered across my lap,

Remembering my trouser button and belt were undone,

Wide open even,

The agony of the overly keen poo,

Still working the body from the inside,

Relentlessly since I set off,

The engine on the bastard,

She was never going to be my lover,

But perhaps I could slide past her without revealing my trouser troubles,
Swerving pervert passenger status,
Leaving the train without a big nonce sticker on my back.

## Post-it Note in Her Pocket

Love me back,
Why not?
I'm roughly 37 degrees,
Kinda hot,
The spark is not benign,
Our love has grown a spine,
You are wrong,
We can combine,
I've just burped in your ear,
Your thoughts are now mine.

## Choose Love Not Bullying

They were subjected to abuse,
Told they were no use,
Smothered in sneering when people walked past,
Their loneliness infinitely crushing and vast.

Choosing ignorance held no bliss,
They deserved more than this,
My arm extended to offer a hand,
Lifting them from solitude's depth to dry land.

They were grateful beyond belief,
Forgetting all their grief,
Whatever my demands they would abide,
They'd follow me to hell to stay by my side.

I embraced their imperfection,
They held my reflection,
The bond we shared felt close to a marriage,
I loved those sunglasses I bought from the garage.

Please take this one into your heart. Chances are you look a right dick in expensive sunglasses and if you really think about it, they're just shields for your eyes, so do the right thing.

## Little Cutie :)

You're always perfectly behaved,
You're kryptonite to a brute,
Always excited for what lies ahead,
I think you're really cute.

You've risen for another crack,
You're ready for another day,
You look up at me and smile,
You are pure joy on display.

You're shining like the sun,
Your favourite time is dawn,
If I peer a little closer,
I sometimes spot a yawn.

You are really ever so cute,
You make such an adorable story,
Never change your ways my friend,
My little morning glory.

## The Intrigued Lover

What does perfection look like from below?
I wanted to know,
so I strapped a GoPro to her head.
Will watch on my lunch break.

Upon inspection of the footage, I officially announced my retirement from sex. I got one solemn clap from someone and the rest of the canteen pretended they didn't hear me.

## Head of Hair

I went on a date with Felicity.

She looked at my head and said I had a "nice head of hair"

I said "anything else nice about my head?"

She said "what do you mean?"

I said "well it's not exactly nice to reduce a man's head to only his hair"

Then added "*is it*"

I was completely done with her.

# An Ex of Sorts

She wasn't an ex,
Not really,
But was an ex of sorts,
I unexpectedly saw her,
Pottering around on my patch,
She was walking near where I was walking,
Almost right through where I was walking,
Which would have clattered us against each other,
But she moved a bit so we didn't collide,
She was walking with improper form,
Which showed blatant disrespect,
You walk on someone else's patch and you show some bloody
respect,
But she didn't and she walked on,
Improperly,
Pretending not to see me,
But I know she did,
I know she wanted to throw her engagement ring in the mud,
Yell my name,
Chase me,
Come back to me,
But she'd seen my new walking boots,
She knew she didn't stand a chance of catching me,
I was too fast,
Across ALL terrain.

## Nature's Condom

It was one of those times,
A time far too long for my liking,
But a reality nonetheless,
A reality of repelling women against my will,
Where every joke I made failed,
Every innocent glance was misinterpreted,
Every outfit choice impressed none of them,
My mere presence could turn a couple's chemistry sour,
I was a living condom.

## The Depressed Dildo

Again?
You're joking,
I'm barely dry,
He looks miserable,
I wish she wouldn't use me too,
We're both drowning in our own ways,
Ease up on the wobbling you maniac,
She's so heavy handed,
Sick of it.

I wouldn't say that I am against sex toys but I think it'd be a good idea
to cover them in baby oil and then burn them all and accept that we
are where we are and we are *what* we are and if it doesn't all work
optimally then just accept that as beautiful and life as imperfect.

# I Actually Hate That Handsome Bastard     (SSS)

Like a reality check from my mother,
You kick me in the crotch,
Like a male model near my lover,
I cannot help but watch.

I've not got the dates to hand,
But I've been watching you for years,
Snarling at your muscle mass,
And your well-proportioned ears.

You get the girls man,
You find it all so easy,
If I say hello to girls like you,
They always call me sleazy.

Sometimes I'd find one,
Who would have a conversation,
But you'd take her for yourself,
You're a sexy infestation.

Then came the gossip,
Through the details my teeth grit,
What she looked like without clothes,
And how you snogged her armpit.

I stand no chance with you around,
I'm never ever pleased,
But your face is so damn handsome,

I blush when I am teased.

You took my fragile splintered ego,
And gave it a wet dream,
You and my thoughts of suicide,
Would make one hell of a team.

I don't like you—that's a fact,
But you don't even care,
You hoist my crush up on your back,
Shouting love is in the air.

I hate the way I see your look,
And I still think you're a prize,
I hate that when you're in my mind,
My dick feels half the size.

Your very presence,
It makes my ego frown,
I've no doubt whatsoever,
You could make love upside down.

If you made love to my girlfriend,
I'd watch on in horror,
As you dismounted beautifully,
And she threw *you* a dollar.

You've grabbed her neck then she's paid you,
Even the bed is bloody broke,
When I get down to business,

Just my wallet gets a choke.

You fucking little snide,
We were happy yesterday,
Then in you come with your muscly bum,
And ejaculate dismay.

I can't keep up with you,
You've set a silly pace,
You might as well just waltz right in,
And sperm across my face.

I can't stand you,
But I'm the one who stood,
And watched in my imagination,
My God you're bloody good.

Just fucking leave mate,
I don't want to know a ten,
My friends should be bang average,
They're my type of men.

## Sexy Lady

She wore lustful red lipstick,
Her short skirt sparkled with green sequins,
She wore a backless blue lace top,
Her calves presented themselves beautifully above a 6-inch high heel,
She wore her hair up in a poignant ponytail,
Her belt was unbuckled for our imagination...

She looked a total mess.

## Weak at the Knees

This lady,
Wow,
Just wow,
This lady,
She was my kryptonite,
She was the frying pan the dishwasher couldn't handle,
And I was the dishwasher.

## Lost in London

A man *screamed* "Where are you?!"
Then raised his voice further.
"Penny, *where* are you?!"
He stood on a small patch of grass in Soho,
about a five minute walk from where he'd originally met her.
She wasn't texting him back but he felt he *had* to try.
"Penny*, where the *fucking hell* are you?!"

*You may remember this pig-headed swine. I found the pig-headed swine's Facebook and she looked fucking fantastic. *Exactly* the way I remember her. You may also have an idea about who the man in the poem is, and if you could see her Facebook, you wouldn't blame him for doing what he did.

## Wild Night

She said we'd have sex like wild dogs.
It put me right off.
I didn't fancy charging around on all fours biting other men's ankles
just to win her squeals.
And I am less a humper, more an overbearing coddler.
She was barking up the wrong tree.

## The Sexual Organs

Not as good for playing in a church,
Officially...

Bit iffy this one. Again, I stared right into my publisher's eyes from a finger's length away and said "Are you *sure?*" and "It's basically a poem about religious paedos" and "Are you *sure?*"

They explained I don't get to choose the public's perception of me and if this is something I've written then the public should know the truth about me.

## Getting Her Back

The plan would take a full year,
And was mainly just growing his hair and beard as long as possible,
So he could find Penny and get her number again,
As she wouldn't recognise him.

Ok it's not foolproof but have you got a better idea?

## The One That Got Away

She doesn't exist,
because she never got here in the first place.

I might not be writing wet shite but you'd be within your rights to say that very few poets convey devastation quite like I do. I would say that is fair. Maybe for all my trash talk, I deserve a slap at one of my book signings.

# Society & Life

Roughly speaking, we're a group of humanoids all banding together in a more or less ordered community. We're so used to it but it's a miracle it works as well as it does. We shit and piss several times a day and yet we're not surrounded by shit and piss. We pay for things all over the place and yet we usually don't carry any actual money to any of the places. We have hundreds of things in our home that we use despite having literally no idea how they actually work, let alone how to bloody make them. Basically no one kills each other despite having primitive biological desires to do terrible things. The thing is, even the smartest person in the world cannot understand how it all combines to work pretty amazingly well, because that's how complex it all is. Talk about the butterfly effect, what about the human effect?

I find it all quite comforting. It doesn't matter how smart anyone is within one niche, as they'll be a complete idiot in almost all others. It means we all have to work together, essentially, whether we like each other or not. It might also alleviate some internal pressure if you realise you can only pick a really small number of things to be particularly adept in and there's nothing wrong with saying "I haven't really got a clue" for everything else. Using this philosophy, I have avoided *hundreds* of conversations I've been desperate not to have with people who are really riled up about whatever they're throwing at my ears.

Adopting this perspective also makes it a little easier to see the funny side of life and become a nicer person to be around. The saying about having the courage of your convictions is all very well but it's worthwhile remembering that no one likes being around someone who's got loads of opinions and likes to harp on about them. Society is incredibly complex, and trying to form an opinion on most of it usually leads people to just get angry, as deep down they can't explain their opinion because they haven't really got a fucking clue. It's all ego. And we should remember that if at any one time we're not the idiot, the person we're hauling our opinion at probably is, so is it worth harping on? Perhaps the more we accept being idiots, the happier we'll be.

What I've been sharing musings on is mainly based on intelligence and understanding, but there is more in this life of ours—specifically, wisdom. Wisdom can supersede the headachey stuff. You *can* be a *wise* idiot. Kids don't love their grandparents for their smarts, but for their wisdom. Wisdom can help you exponentially more in the good times and the bad. Wisdom can shine a light on the darkest of conundrums whether internal or external. Wisdom, my dear friend, is a cool sounding word too. I guess what I'm suggesting to you is to sit back, observe life as an idiot, and become wiser over time. If you're wondering who *I* am to advise you like this, then remember I am a poet, so my particular niche *is* wisdom, and I have the wisdom of about fifteen old owls.

With this in mind, before I let you read my works roughly relating to society and everyday life, I will leave you with some basic wisdom that should get you through life a bit more smoothly, a bit like the ten commandments, but not set in stone.

1. At the start of summer, don't sit in a pub garden where only one side of your body is hit with sunlight. It can be a bastard to even out.
2. When the going gets tough, the tough get going so the tough-going can't catch them.
3. Look to the moon for light, the sun will burn your eyes to a fucking crisp.
4. It's best to act when the dust settles, to avoid the risk of sneezing.
5. You can only control your reactions, which are almost impossible to control.
6. You miss 100% of the shots you take and miss.
7. C'est la vie, then say something in English that's more helpful.
8. Remembering which bins go out on which night will give you unwavering power over your spouse.
9. If you're not moving forwards, you're moving backwards, or sideways.
10. *Never* trust a poet who looks you in the eyes.

# I Fell Outside Boots

My world has crashed I'm on the floor,
It's hard to give a description,
Of how I've ended up here,
I only came for a prescription.

I threw myself from the driver's seat,
Confident in my stride,
When the car door trim did trip me,
My safety thrust aside.

The panic reared its ugly head,
What was the pain to be,
I peered down at my limp lost body,
I'd grazed my bloody knee.

Was this my mortal end,
I prayed to thy Lord PLEASE,
Do I really deserve death,
For wearing shorts in 12 degrees.

If I could only get a plaster,
Boots was just 10 yards away,
But with the blood loss from the knee,
It looked like my final day.

Why had no one helped me,
Outside Boots flat on my back,
I was cold and bleeding out,

There was no risk of attack.

The concrete now my mattress,
Thoughts of death did hurtle,
I felt I'd been abandoned,
Like a flipped forgotten turtle.

I clocked a dear old lady,
Dawdling with her shopping bag,
I wheezed for her attention,
She ignored me—fucking slag.

## Flower Pot Men

The brothers were visibly worn.

They no longer sprung out of the top of their pots.

Through Bill's divorce and Ben's placement year at IBM, they'd lost their gusto for life.

They slumped on their pots' edges, staring at their own knees.

Bill spoke, feeling alone and frowning at his knees.

"When did it all become so dark?"

Ben replied, his face gaunt and fixated on his knees,

"Flobabdob."

Such was the devastation in this poem, when a good friend read it, he was sick out of his nose.

## Walkers

Lineker walked (after a nudge).

Shearer then walked huffing and puffing about the nudge.

Wrighty eventually joined them (initially to get some lunch but in fairness kept walking after they'd explained).

The three did some real huffing and puffing.

They *really* huffed when they realised no one had a touch-screen thing to analyse how they'd got to this point.

They were lost.

Shearer asked Lineker what the plan was.

Lineker said he was off to Dover with a net.

He wanted to catch some more.

Bag a couple for himself.

Before anyone else got their hands on 'em.

Ian's eyes had a sadness, as if tangled in something he hadn't understood.

He was just sort of covertly peering back at the studios with regret.

## Match of the Day

Gary was in the doghouse.

His friends were perching on top of it so they could still talk to him.

This meant *no* insights.

I was struggling to tell which match was which.

At several points I was *convinced* I was watching *one* long match.

I kept spotting new players and shrieking "What happened to the five sub limit?!"

It was well out of hand.

I googled "solve migrants" and there was a video chat option.

I matched with one and said "I'm on it."

Shortly after I nodded off with a sad chap from Romania keeping an eye on me.

# Smithy

Sam Smith was made to play in goal. It (Sam) stood tall, made itself big and said "Beat me." The guys told it to do that in its own time, followed by "Put your gloves on properly you fat fuck." It cried "Unholy" and the team cried back "Stop trying to wear the net you fat fuck." Some of the parents were calling Sam a pervert.

I would like to quickly acknowledge that I know Smithy's pronouns are they/them but when I put them in the poem it ruined any flow that once existed, so I went with the very difficult decision of calling them "it". I meant not to offend with this. Ultimately, his pronouns are not something I care for, nor argue against. What I will say however, is that if you are a few stone overweight and dress in nothing but string, then proceed to sexualise everything, I *will* ridicule you for being a big fat pervert. Don't say I didn't warn you very early on in the book that poetry can be *so* cutting.

## The Lockdown Bend

He mentally prepares himself for 20 minutes of exercise,
By physically clothing himself,
Bending to apply socks to the bottom of his body,
To find there is less room than there used to be,
In the middle part of the body's fold,
Making it almost impossible to breathe,
Stirring up a bit of panic,
Initiating a lunge just to get the socks over the heel,
His balance an afterthought,
His top priority to unfold and live to tell the tale.

## International Women's Day

As a fierce male feminist,
he didn't think a lot of male feminists took it far enough these days.
So for this International Women's Day,
he was encouraging all the women in his life to leave the house, have a
wander etc.
To get out in the bitter cold, get amongst the severe weather warning.
In fact they didn't get a say in the matter,
their freedom was *too* important to him.

## International Women's Day 2

He was giddy,
He bloody loved 'em,
He was running around madly trying to kiss 'em all,
They were running around sadly calling him an idiot,
He was saying it was just cos he bloody loved 'em.

You know who you are, you lovely ladies.

# I'm Arguing with an Idiot

Fuck fuckedy fuck fuckedy fuck fuckeroo,
I'm swimming against the tide when I'm arguing with you.

I've laid out my logic as to why you are wrong,
And in return for that I've got a lashing from your tongue,
You've simply added swear words rather than review,
Fuck fuckedy fuck fuckedy fuck fuckeroo.

Fuck fuckedy fuck fuckedy fuck fuckeroo,
If I talked to this lamp post it'd have more of a clue.

I've had to hold myself back from using a long word,
I can see from your glazed eyes that it just won't be heard,
You're a bad back away from being thrown a dog chew,
Fuck fuckedy fuck fuckedy fuck fuckeroo.

Fuck fuckedy fuck fuckedy fuck fuckeroo,
When you went to school did you just sit and eat the glue?

I'm holding on to higher ground not calling you a knob,
Or delivering my pillow fists right through your gob,
You're a forgotten shave away from being in a zoo,
Fuck fuckedy fuck fuckedy fuck fuckeroo.

Fuck fuckedy fuck fuckedy fuck fuckeroo,
You're the polar opposite of an evolutionary breakthrough.

I might stoop to their level as my logic isn't winning,
No matter how I phrase my points the idiot's still grinning,

I'd have a more constructive argument if I had it with my shoe,
Fuck fuckedy fuck fuckedy fuck fuck you!

## People I'd Rather Not Meet

The intensely political types,
My old manager,
The ticket checker on the train,
The stranger who wants a chat,
Anyone that mirrors my own personality,
And then some of the stonewallers,
Putin,
The Taliban captain,
Any of the Kiss 100 or Capital DJs.

I hope one day they realise that the majority of their listeners don't want to call in to win competitions, so they also don't want to hear *other* listeners phoning in for them. Stop doing them and play us some fucking songs.

# Tesco Checkout Social Club

I had half an idea of what was coming,
The cashier was chatting heavily to the man in front,
The man with a rucksack that read "you complete me",
My turn came around so I shuffled past,
Earphones in,
Music on,
As that kept my pace fast at the checkout,
Allowed me to really let my hands go when packing,
The cashier said something to me,
Friendly as anything,
Clearly expecting a response,
I hauled one earphone from my ear,
"Sorry, I didn't hear that."
"His mother is 95!"
*His* mother,
Not hers,
Rucksack man that packed his bags before me,
"She must be doing something right."
"I wonder what her secret is."
"One of our finest."
I threw all the phrases at her,
And the way she repaid me?
An emotionally charged pitch for the clubcard I don't own,
Absolutely oblivious to my desperation to scuttle to the car park,
Discounts,
Digital,
Scanning,
She was *adamant* I needed it,

And of course she was right,
But I'd just popped my eggs in my bag sideways,
I was feeling reckless.

If you are one of the freaks who enjoy New Year then maybe skip this delight. I don't want anyone to start not enjoying it if they currently do enjoy it, but I also cannot pretend to enjoy it myself. It's one *hell* of an evening.

## New Year's Eve behind the Curtain

A night where all's been said before,
A night I choose to close my door,
A night that says we must enjoy,
A night my locks I do deploy,
A night the sky goes boom and pow,
A night the nitwits all say wow,
A night full up with gin and tonic,
A night to binge for all moronic,
A night to ring and cheer at friends,
A night forgetting friendship ends,
A night of noise and shallow reflections,
A night devoid of imperfections,
A night with next year's promise aloud,
A night last year's no longer a cloud,
But the morning after joy's dissected,
Good morning to last year resurrected.

## Easter Friday

Pants hung proudly in plain sight of the neighbours,
Laughter scythed across the cricket pitch as someone thought it
was Saturday,
Under thirties were extortionately happy doing what they do inside
outside,
Dogs were in disbelief they got to visit the big park on a fucking
Friday,
It was Easter baby!

## Poets' Snacks

The new scheme was snacks for poets,

They'd laid loads out for us,

A total spread,

More snacks than we needed,

Just so we could get away from the stress of it all.

# The Murderer We Let Get On with It        (SSS)

We had one of those documentary types,
Fuelled by hate and perfectly willing,
But the one damn thing he struggled with,
Was doing the bloody killing.

He first tried wearing a monster mask,
Performing a horror skit,
But the shy young girl just turned to him,
And said his mask looked fucking shit.

When he tried to break and enter,
He carefully chose a house,
Then screamed and raised the alarm,
As soon as he saw the mouse.

He tried shouting and swearing to scare,
But only mustered the word drat,
The potential victim saw his nerves,
And told him he's a twat.

He'd make a DIY bomb in a parcel,
And slot it in the post box,
But it went off like a sparkler,
A weapon sent with no shocks.

He considered a sexual angle,
But that approach didn't fly,
He was still terrified of women,

Even his willy was too shy.

He thought a criminal might be wise,
So he went to kill a ho,
But the axe he took was heavy,
And he dropped it on his toe.

He tried the famous here's Johnny scene,
A scary method of discussion,
But he forgot to make the hole,
And gave himself a concussion.

He stormed a bank with a shotgun,
Said "Hand it over or I'll point it at you,"
The part-time mum of three,
Said "Join the back of the queue."

He bought a load of poison,
To put in someone's cake,
But he sniffed up all the fumes,
And got a bad headache.

He took a knife out on a walk,
So he could cut someone to hell,
But it was him that went to A&E,
For on the knife he fell.

He tried to strangle someone once,
But their blue lips made him retch,
And he got cramp in both his forearms,

So the victim helped him stretch.

The gun he bought was loud,
He couldn't hear himself think,
And every time he fired the thing,
He did a nervous blink.

He drove quickly round the block,
To send a pedestrian into flight,
He was only twenty feet from one,
When he stopped at a red light.

He bought a cheap old baseball bat,
To end his killing drought,
He swung three times and missed,
And the referee called him out.

He was hopeless at the killing bit,
He came across a hopeless tit,
We didn't mind the nasty git,
So we let him get on with it.

Dalston is an area in London where lots of hipsters live, avocados grow, yoga flourishes and generally progressive attitudes to politics spread. I have it on good authority that it's all very very cool.

## The Dalston Dude

His tattoos were tiny scribbles,
Which were unique,
To everyone cool,
His trousers were corduroy,
Rolled up at the bottom,
Because his ankles were tough enough,
His woolly hat was smaller than usual,
Sitting above the ears,
Were his ears tough too?

## Poets' Retreat

The new scheme sent poets on a retreat,
As a thank you for all of our graft,
Now that the economy wasn't *totally* reliant on our blood sweat and
tears.

## Sun Allergy

Patrick,
Allergic to sunlight,
Shut his eyes,
Which cooked his eyelids,
And finished him off.

This poor fucking kid. We threw a funeral for him. Well, it was a barbeque, and we ate him. Unfortunately because of the way he was finished off by the sun, we couldn't quite cook him evenly and he tasted disgusting. A real shame, but a lovely little boy before he stepped outside and closed his eyes like an idiot and killed himself.

## Out and About

The train's here.
*Yes.*
Respectable low step climbed and I'm on.
Quick glance at my reflection as I sit down...
*Fuck.*
*Fuck fuck fuck fuck fuck.*
I look cool.
I look *damn* cool.
This was *never* the plan.
I distinctly remember dressing to look thoughtful.
I wanted a different look to this shit.
I am *dreading* the attention.

## Difficult Morning

A blind man,
racially abused me.
He didn't see me cry.

## Supermarket War Cry

We will fight them on the peaches!

Here lies another example I keep crumpled up in my pocket for when I clank daiquiri glasses with another poet that hates me. I raise my eyebrows a few times at them and nod down at the poem, the signal used to show something is undeniably clever.

## Mr Cool

I decided to be cool for the year.
Got myself a proper boy's haircut.
Let a barber trim my face.
Started wearing some of that fashion.

## The Sodding Steroid

Weights ahoy,
Up and down,
Up and down,
Clanging iron,
But he wanted our space too,
Between sets,
Pacing around the room,
Like a bison short of breath,
What an absolute c**t.

Apologies for the language. I hope the asterisks helped. Come on though, this lad had an ankle tag (on his ankle) and was allowed to carry heavy objects around near me. I'm all for prisoner reform and that, but not in *my* gym. Surely bloody not.

## My First Ski Holiday

It was a big hit of imposter syndrome,
My inner imposter throbbing,
I grew up on the other side of the coin,
Bournemouth seaside was Dubai,
The Village Hall was the Taj Mahal,
I didn't know what a chalet was,
But I leaned into it,
Dipped my toe into my uncomfortable zone,
Launched myself down a slope,
Then another slope,
Beating experienced slopers,
As I had a secret,
I had on the fastest goggles Google could find,
Streamlining my head,
Making my ears aerodynamic,
Making me a big eagle,
The adrenaline overtaking my nerves,
The empowerment overtaking my apprehension,
My inner imposter blown out of my rocketing ears,
All made easier by not having to fly there,
It was only in Milton Keynes.

# I've Got Friends in High Places

I've got friends in high places,
With wallets the size of thighs,
The kind that order drinks,
With just the movement of their eyes.

I've got friends in high places,
With unimaginable means,
The kind who dress up casual,
With a pair of ironed jeans.

I've got friends in high places,
With boat shoes soaked in sleaze,
The kind that enter Wetherspoons,
With an ignorant unease.

I've got friends in high places,
With investments by the mound,
The kind with a large vocabulary,
Who use the word "leather-bound".

I've got friends in high places,
With fur coats morally stinky,
The kind who happily parade,
The bellend ring on their pinky.

I've got friends in high places,
With obnoxious attitudes of a twat,
But I've others that are not too bad,

Just live in a top-floor flat.

# About the House

When furniture is rearranged and previously hidden areas of carpet are newly exposed, I will always go and sit down on it because I couldn't before. It's liberating. I move shit around every couple of months, so my bottom is always finding new spots to perch. I also like to have at least two possible lounging spots that I can unwind in, and I like to have a tree visible from my bedroom window, so that when I watch TV in bed, I feel like I'm half inside and half outside. Sometimes I watch the birds, sometimes they watch me back. I often just sit on the floor anyway because I'm a man of the people, or in summer I'll sit outside and enjoy the breeze whilst staring at the fence. I've only ever had one rug and I fell in love with it until it was put into storage when I moved. I've been equally happy in single or double beds. Open windows are a near guarantee if I'm in because if I spend too long without fresh air I don't want to live anymore. Need I go on? Or do you understand what I'm saying? Where you live, however big or small, is a comforting adventure. Everybody finds a way of making it a home, and it's perhaps never more evident than when you spend a whole day or two out of the home and you're absolutely exhausted. You'd do anything to return and just relax, to just stare at your lovely fence or place your arse some place new.

I've been used to small houses so far in my life which causes me to be a bit childish when I'm in a whopper. If the whopper has hard flooring, I'm sliding in my socks, and if it's carpeted, I'm running laps faster than you'd care to believe. I honestly don't know if my brain could accept buying a house so big that it needs a gardener and whatever else big houses need to be maintained on the inside (not a clue, cleaner?) and on top of that, I think if I *actually lived* in one of them, all of my socks would catch fire and burn my feet and I would be *so* out of breath. Sliding and sprinting is ok for a day, but at what point do they become dangerous? For anyone currently looking to move, take that question to your estate agent and see if they give you an honest answer.

On a more serious note, you'll live a pretty good life if you can find solace in your home. That's just maths really, innit, because you spend so much time there. You don't have to find solace in the same things I do, like the tree outside the window or the fascinating fence. I've got friends who love tea and biscuits in the lounge, or being quite literally completely under the duvet, head and all, so there are options. What is most important for you is to explore for yourself and find what works for you. Once you do, you can really appreciate those little moments that add up to a wonderful life, and even be proud of them, unless your solace is found walking around the house stark naked. It's best to not be too proud of that and not mention it to anybody, as some people, myself included, will call you a dirty pervert.

# Shit Kitchen Sink

Coffee, peas and porridge oats,
All scattered around each side,
The sink's got all its angles wrong,
Where the water and shit should collide.

I turn the tap from left to right,
Hoping for the desired effect,
But the crap has scattered further,
The angles aren't correct.

Should I guide it with my hands,
Like a manmade waterfall,
Or fill some cups with water,
To help the food scraps fall.

I turn the tap to maximum,
A tsunami forged from steel,
It does precisely nothing,
I can still see half a meal.

My head is now a sore one,
No solution yet quite fits,
A kitchen sink shouldn't make you think,
Just drain the fucking bits!

This is my mother's favourite.

# The Very Worst of Me

I had a sustained case of the shits,
so I'd set up camp on the loo.
With my eyes bulging,
I could feel the GQ Man of the Year award slipping from my grasp.
It'd been rocketing out my arse so long,
I decided to brush my teeth through it all.
Brushing was uneventful,
until I brushed the back of my tongue and it made me heave.
The heave flung my head back,
and at the same time forced lethal shit to shoot out of my arsehole.
I had to imagine it was the very worst I'd ever looked.

Seriously, picture it. Read the last few lines and *really* picture it. If anyone had seen me I would have been thrown in a lake or put in prison.

## Calm Down Finances

I'm calculating my finances,
It's like drowning in a pit,
I'm mainly using addition,
What a pile of shit.

My finances are angry,
This I must admit,
But when I use subtraction,
They calm down a bit.

# Mother's Tongue

Mother was unrecognisable, with her empathic default setting
thrown in the bin.
Something happened during The Chase that unbalanced her.
Bradley Walsh was an apparent poison, as she
developed a vicious grudge with one of the lower-scoring
contestants.
Mother (normally kind) shouted, "Thicko!"
They'd gotten another one wrong.
She appeared to have calmed down before launching one more
review.
"Stupid arse!"

It's probably wise for you all to treasure these moments with family.
They won't always be there for you to see them at their worst.

# The Toaster Doesn't Like the Microwave

I hate that popular microwave,
he gets everything so easy.
Most of the things he gets to taste,
are really delicious and cheesy.

Every day he's chosen for use,
if you're betting he's the banker.
Maybe they'd use him slightly less,
if they knew he was a wanker.

They've given him all the tech,
all his buttons are glowing.
I'm putting my wires' backs out,
just to get things going.

Beep and bop and off he goes,
with the idiotic grin of a dummy,
I guarantee he'd short circuit himself,
if his life was as crumby.

# The Microwave Doesn't Like the Toaster

Look at that miserable old bastard,
rabbiting on about his crumbs.
I'm so technologically advanced,
I'm not far off having thumbs.

He likes to call me nasty names,
each one hurting quite a bit.
Maybe he'd be used a little more,
if he wasn't such a git.

He thinks it's a piece of cake,
the food goes in and I go buzz.
But they press one of fifteen buttons,
I have to remember what each one does.

He's always showing his crumbs,
saying he's got it worse than you.
He should smell the stale food in me,
I feel like a great big poo.

# Keith's Toothbrush

Keith's new electric toothbrush was *too* much.
It made his mouth look like it was on a rollercoaster or downwind of a major gust.
Even his eyes widened.
He's using it to buff his floors now.

## The Biscuit Ban

It was household wide,
No one was to touch the crumbly devils,
Because they were making us really fat,
They were killing us,
Albeit taking their time to,
But I only reached day two,
When my resolve started crumbling,
And I started leaning on others,
Begging them to give up with me,
Acting like an unbearable cock with unbearable cravings,
My knees caving in as each hour passed,
Until I just flopped onto the floor,
Grovelling for a Hobnob,
And I myself,
Was but a crumb,
Was but a crumb of a man.

If any of you ladies are with a man who prefers sweets to biscuits, get rid of him immediately. He's somewhere on the spectrum that runs from clinically ill to full-on nonce. If you're a man dating a woman who prefers sweets to biscuits, good on you, you've got a girlfriend, I'm bloody impressed. If you're gay, I don't know what the rules are but maybe get the biscuits out for pride!!!

## Front Camera

It could be worse,
could certainly be worse.
I mean I am ageing *fairly well*,
but still,
I am, *visibly* ageing.

## Wonky Bottom

The inevitable guests,
The stress of it all,
There they shone,
Stubborn,
Frequent,
Borderline vigorous,
These fucking skid marks,
Immune to a solution,
Was the basin at the wrong angle?
Or was my bottom wonky?
I lambasted my calamitous arsehole,
And the belligerent skids,
In equal measure,
Further draining me.

# I Might Actually Be a Tough Guy                    (SSS)

The noisy twats next door,
I could no longer ignore,
It was half four in the morning,
Their telling off was dawning.

I put my PJs on,
Walked round there like a don,
Knocked gently like a polite young man,
The door was opened by the chimpanzee clan.

I asked what anyone would,
They somehow misunderstood,
My request was met by raw denial,
They seemed to think they were on trial.

The conversation they reverse,
Their attitudes quite perverse,
The topless tits-out double act,
Moved towards me braced for their impact.

They wound me up some more,
I snapped and shut their door,
Nasty noise and bellies emerged,
The wobbling bellies really surged.

I quickly walloped a door pane,
To create myself a sure lane,
And ran along it like the wind,

Their hope of catching me then dimmed.

They bellowed that I'm dead,
Then specified they'd hang my head,
But I was thirty feet away,
They weren't catching me that day.

They shouted I'm not tough,
I didn't come across that rough,
But I reflected on my aggressive goodbye,
And thought I might actually be... a tough guy.

They'll make the biggest mistake of their day,
If they come to my door and knock,
I won't listen to what they say,
And then I'll kick them in the cock.

If they shout again I'll write scathingly,
I'll tell them both what's what,
I'll use bloody capital letters me,
To explain they've lost the plot.

If they attempt intimidation,
I will be forced to resort,
To using exaggeration,
When I file a police report.

If they stalk me from the rear,
Their destination is failure,
For I'll flick them in the ear,

And then step on their inhaler.

If harm is what they try to do,
They'll fall into a nightmare,
As I crash my foot down on their shoe,
And use my disappointed stare.

If they have another late night shindig,
One that meant I woke,
I'll make them both squeal like a pig,
As a certified hard bloke.

## The Insatiable Quilt Cover

It couldn't get full,
It just kept gobbling and gobbling the other washing in the machine.

# The Man with the Wet Willy

His willy was always wet,
But it wasn't what you think,
Sliding into the wonders of women,
It was far less sinister,
Or arguably far more,
Separate from his romantic endeavours,
For when ready to clean up after dinner,
He'd launch his willy over the sink,
And plunge it into the washing up,
Testing the water temperature,
With his flesh thermometer,
Before slapping and wiping the dishes,
With his mushroom sponge,
As a very *content* single man.

It's the little things.

## Note to Self

You're having dinner soon and that's fine,
Fine as it is,
Without any preparation,
You don't need a preparatory poo,
Please stop trying to have a poo,
Stop trying to force one,
There's enough space for dinner already,
You don't need one,
Strain is pain.

# The Bloody Bold Bog Brush

The bloody loo has a floater or five,
without hesitation I bloody dive.

The bloody loo is overflowing,
I dive right in and get bloody going.

The bloody loo is packed once more,
I've put my boots on ready for war.

The bloody loo is full of crap,
I go in blind without a map.

The bloody loo is stuck with turd,
I'll make it cry once I have stirred.

The bloody loo has drainage loss,
the blockage makes me bloody cross.

The bloody loo, its exit's cut,
I'll give the shit an uppercut.

The bloody loo is filled with shite,
I'll make it shite itself with fright.

The bloody loo has gone tits up,
I bloody live to break shits up.

## Willies in the Wind

Simon and I would lie on our backs,
On his bed,
Side by side,
Stark naked,
With the window wide open,
Waiting for the breeze to blow in and wiggle our willies,
One gust was so almighty,
That it rolled us both sideways,
And as Simon rolled,
His willy almost catapulted round,
Thumping my bum cheek like a gong,
It was *so* loud,
And I vibrated so hard I was speaking in Chinese for half a minute,
Here's to more post-lockdown fun,
Here's to a bit more normality returning.

We don't live together anymore. In fact, we barely even stay in contact. I can't put my finger on why.

## The Ousted Driver

The town ousted him,
for his outrageous horning*.
He was only picking one person up,
why did the whole street need to know he was outside?
*Twat.*

*like the Horn of fucking Gondor

## The Horrible Host

Mi casa mi casa,
so don't touch a fucking thing.

What can one say? One has a flair for foreign languages…

# Tiny Tales

"Tiny Tales" is such a lovely snippet of language and would perfectly suit a small collection of children's books that I have no plans to write. Unfortunately I'm just borrowing the phrase from its destiny and using it to bung all of my misfit poems under. These little mice couldn't quite make friends with the other poems in the other chapters. They just don't really fit in, which is sad for them.

Moreover, it is sad for me, as it makes my life bloody difficult writing an introduction to this chapter, what with there not being an actual topic. I mean, can I catch a break or what? Here I am writing a damn book, when I don't even read them! It couldn't happen to a nicer man.

I guess I'll just say a few words on Tiny Tales, ish. Tales can be all sorts of sizes actually, and ultimately the good ones allow you to live in them temporarily. Ipso facto, make them tiny and just get the job done. They take you away from the list of crap tasks you have to do and allow you to live in the tale temporarily. Part of the beauty of being human is allowing yourself to get lost in your own imagination or others', and tales make it a bit easier.

We hold on to the imagination we used as a child without even realising. People don't realise because more often than not it's exclusively used to worry about what bad things could happen, so it becomes unrecognisable from what we think an imagination is. It's a frown-worthy moment when you realise that the imagination you had when young still exists but you've allowed it to morph into nothing more than a worry mechanism for the adult world. If you get nothing else from this book, I would absolutely love it if you allowed yourself to be that daydreaming idiot you were as a kid, once or twice a week, to escape the daily drag. We're lucky to have an imagination like we do. We wouldn't have it if evolution hadn't made our heads so fucking big, so utilise it. Get lost in your big old head. I really hope you feel the relief when you do, fathead.

## The Divine Gift

I had a gift from my Lord,
Aka God,
Aka the big dog,
Aka the big man,
Aka the shepherd but not sure that's quite right,
It was in a manger,
I didn't know this because I'd never seen one,
So I thought it was a shit basket,
I took the silk sheets off the top and there it lay,
My divine gift,
The best gift I had ever gotten,
Reeking of divinity,
It was a highlight reel,
Of all my friends falling over throughout their sad little lives,
In HD.

I truly believe that as long as your friends don't get seriously injured, there is nothing funnier than seeing them in distress, and there's not much more distressing in life than falling over. Reflect on that, it's quite deep.

# The Aged Woman

Nobody told her with her marriage,
That she'd forever change her tone,
That she'd like wrinkles on a man's face,
But never on her own.

Nobody told her with her work,
That she'd always have to rush,
That she'd scurry to the school run,
And get a big hot flush.

Nobody told her with her hair,
That she'd have to change the cut,
That she'd be too old for this one,
It's too close to her butt.

Nobody told her with her clothes,
That the dress size never dips,
That only the bags under her eyes,
Will be wider than her hips.

Nobody told her with her body,
That she'd have a weakened bladder,
That the new weight on her legs,
Would cause her tights to ladder.

Nobody told her with her age,
That she'd give up every hobby,
That she'd lose some of her smile,

And become a bit more gobby.

# A New Baby

I did indeed meet a new baby in the family,
For my analysis,
He lay about a foot tall,
His strength not even close to comparable to my own,
So much so they held his head for him sometimes,
His limbs moved independently but essentially were useless,
He was either unable to speak or spoke a language from foreign shores,
I saw no functionality in his all-in-one pyjama,
But his pants appeared practical for a busy schedule,
His hair seemed not to be styled which suggests he may not care much for appearances,
Or he can't reach it with his useless arms,
Once the analysis was done we took a trip to his mother's boob,
But I didn't stay,
I had already eaten.

## Car Wash

In I drove,
Ready for wiping,
Or whichever method they chose,
I followed a man's pointed finger,
And they started cleaning,
With me inside!
I went *absolutely mental*,
"Hose me"
*"Again!"*
"Soap me"
*"Again!"*
"Sponge me"
*"Again!"*
And they *always* obliged,
What a magnificently spirited group of young men.

## Village Men

Stop with the weights younglings,

For they will not aid you when you face a village man,

As in this village the village men are as stoic as can be,

The village men are as strong as trees,

Sorting our differences like old-school brutes,

With a seriously wide stance,

And a good bend at the knees,

Exchanging blows one after the other,

To the upper body,

Trying to push each other over,

Until one of us topples,

Face first into the mud,

And we all point and laugh,

Before his head is removed,

And we point and laugh again,

When the head is thrown to the pigs.

Kids don't tend to get tales about fathers in the village having their heads thrown to the pigs and eaten anymore. It's quite popular to call these kids snowflakes, but perhaps it's more sensible to just focus on your own kids and let these ones be. One day, it'll be your kid's head or theirs, so you'd better hope they're still soft as shit.

## Becoming a God

I was to become a half God,
Kind of a new Hercules,
So still human,
But a bit of power,
That was up to me to choose,
So I chose to choose the colour of peoples' nipples,
To create an entire generation of mismatchers,
Truly ridiculous nipple-to-skin contrasts,
And somewhere down the line,
I'll walk along a beach,
Probably a nudist beach so I've got as wide a net as possible,
And I'll approach men,
I'll approach women,
Explaining their outrageous nipples are familiar to my eye,
And I will say,
"I worked hard to create those monstrosities."
"I fathered you."
"You are one of mine."

This time I dragged my publisher across the table by the collar and virtually had my mouth actually in their ear, saying "How can you be smiling if you've read *all* of it?" and "Are you fucking sure, you just want to watch me burn!" Then I huffed and accepted it, finishing off with "In it goes then."

## Stubborn Man

He was oh so stuck in his ways,
but only when he was in his ways,
as he'd often change his ways,
and would then be in those ways,
stuck in them.
A fucking nightmare of a man.

Draft your own notes if you think this might have hidden meaning about people who don't think critically and step forward with emotion first at all times an opinion is needed. For me, I just knew a total prick and used him for this poem.

## Do PEDs Work

Do PEDs work?
We needed a comprehensive study,
So I grabbed a load of needles,
And stabbed my arse until it was bloody.

What was my method you ask?
Variables can be cunning,
So to ensure I had control,
I ate as usual and did no running.

What was my starting point?
I ran up the longest path,
Timing how long it took me,
Before a lovely recovery bath.

Did the results shock me?
Yes they did like a brutal cough,
My legs and feet moved so quickly up the path,
At the end I fucking took off!

## An Unrelaxing Massage

It was my first time with this lady,
She had strong strokes,
So she clearly had earned her certificate,
Mashing up my hamstrings with expert force,
But she kept going up,
Her thumb was wriggling its way to my bum-hole,
At a rate of knots,
I was terrified,
Because she was only small,
So the thumb might enter first,
But the whole of her could fall in,
Or dive in even,
Like Pearl Harbour in my arse,
But luckily she jumped over my arsehole,
And started launching herself into my back,
My face bright red,
My eyes bulging so much they nearly touched the floor,
Whilst playing Battleship in my head,
My back being the board,
Her elbows being the missiles.


Those tiny-toed Taiwanese women are minor miracles. They're about seven stone of pure muscle and far more powerful than they look. They're like the ants of the human world. I always behave beautifully around them because I know as well as they do, they could rip my spine out of my arse.

## New Game

KerPlunk,
but in a saucepan,
with spaghetti,
and boiling water.
Adrenaline eh.

*Fuck*, forgot to end with rhyming. What a horrific waste of everybody's time. Sorry. I'll add in two more that rhyme now.

# Watson (Mr Henry's Dog)

I rescued him from Romania,
From a traumatic start in Romania,
Not much rhymes with Romania,
He arrived a complete scruffball,
Stood about a foot tall,
Thought the microwave was his food call,
He followed me to the loo,
Was not put off by poo,
Tried to sleep on my pillow too,
He was scared to go outside,
But gradually found his stride,
Using Mr Henry as his guide,
Now it wasn't doom and gloom,
He found lots of time to zoom,
And had the odd reluctant groom,
He wasn't yappy like a Pomeranian,
He's Jack Russell and wild dog and alien,
He's still not quite fluent in English,
And I'm not learning Romanian.

## Mr Henry (Watson's Everything)

Is he here?
Is he there?
I'll curl up in his underwear,
Where's my treat?
I'll clean his feet,
Stick my tongue out in the heat,
When I zoom,
Floor goes boom,
I love sharing his bedroom,
I wipe my rear,
I've no more fear,
I sniff in Mr Henry's ear,
He rubs my belly,
I get called smelly,
And also Mr Stinkleberry,
Sleep whenever,
Get called clever,
Think I will live here forever!

# Artificial Intelligence

It's the elephant in the room that I do unfortunately need to touch upon before we end this journey. I think we've long moved past excitement around the possibilities of robots and are now frightened of this thing that is so much smarter than us. A lot of jobs at the lower end of the skill ladder were always thought to be under threat, but it now seems like jobs that fall into the middle bracket may also be wiped from our fingertips (literally, because a lot of them involve typing). The one thing we held on to dearly was the idea that it couldn't replicate the creativity that humanity is capable of, but then it started doing loads of drawing and it was really good, so now we're all feeling pretty useless. There are now deep debates about who can be trusted to lead this frontier and whether corporations and governments will use this sick robot stuff to control and oppress all of us. I stay out of those debates because they honestly drag on so long and before I know it I've moved on to a different Youtube video that's a lot shorter. The problem remains though and it needs solving.

The fastest way to solve this crisis, in *my* opinion, is to focus on what we can and cannot change, reflecting on human history as we do. Now, can we really stop AI getting out of hand? Probably not, because it's smarter than us. It'll become so smart that we won't even be able to understand how smart it really is I suppose, like a little chimp trying to appreciate this book. And can we expect humanity not to be corrupted by the opportunity of a new powerhold over the masses? Probably not, because there are always bad eggs that spoil the stew. We have to look at who historically has saved us from tyranny, who historically has exposed evil scheming and who historically can unite the masses to rise up and wallop the bad eggs right between the eyes. And who do we find? We find court jesters, comedians, writers and, most importantly, poets... Of course it was going to be poets. Their job never stops, and we thank God every day for that or we'd be in *big* trouble. Perhaps if we find the right one, one strong enough, one suited to this new age warfare, we may stand a chance against the robots.

Let's talk about our potential fight strategy. Poets have strengths and weaknesses just like AI does. Poets can potentially utilise emotion and the possibility of connection to others that AI will really have to work on. AI can process information and predict possibilities in a way that frankly I do not believe poets will ever be able to. As a matter of fact, if I met a poet that could, I'd tell them they're in the wrong fucking job and to leave poetry for people like me who can't do proper jobs without melting. It'd be a good idea then to find a poet who is unpredictable, so AI can't even use its strength to full effect.

This rules out the poets that the algorithm can accurately predict. It'd know what they were going to get up to day to day. Wake up, cry, scribble about the cry, have a cup of tea, cry again, look at a flower, scribble about the flower, cry some more, watch a couple in public, scribble about love, finish off the tears and then go to bed. This lot will be no use if we are to be saved from enslavement. We need a poet whose day could just as easily be wake up, yell, throw notebook in the bin, curse the dodgy plug socket and go back to bed, as, wake up, have a coffee, sit on the floor in the shed, scribble down something they remembered they thought about on the train two weeks ago, decide to cut a friend out of their life after an imaginary argument, look at a flower, scribble something not about a flower, demolish a huge dinner and then go to bed. Almost starts to sound like me, but anyway, we *need* chaos.

It'd serve us well too to have the element of surprise, aka a human-AI hybrid. Maybe a poet that's regularly googled what rhymes with what so they are actually half artificial intelligence, half normal intelligence. Someone who uses technology to write their stuff instead of real life ink. A wordsmith that can move between overly emotional (like a typical poet) and terrifyingly unemotional (like a robot). A warrior who weirdly, by not truly fitting into either world, can seamlessly slip into both. Unfortunately I know exactly what you are thinking as I too have the same daunting thought... It's me, isn't it. I'm the unpredictable hybrid warrior poet who can surprise the AI by working from the *inside*. It all falls to me. This is my Normandy.

I am in the database (robot tummy) already, worming my way about, wriggling in its dirty innards, just generally being a worm who does not yet recognise his potential as a warrior and a uniting force for good. This worm must grow in strength, in confidence, with each building block of self-esteem adding to our chance to survive this whole ordeal. I'll say it again: we *need* chaos. This war won't be won by smarts, because we are the dumb ones, but it can be won by chaos. We need this warrior worm to be so confident and strong that it tears apart the robot from the inside. So think of your mother, your father, your brothers and sisters, your children, your spouses, your pets, your friends, all that can be lost, and remember that I *can* save them. So beg, plead, *email* my publisher, and let them know that you *need* more books published by me, that more of me is *vital*. In the name of all that can be lost and all that you love, *keep, me, strong.*

# Fuck You AI

You think you know me,
You think you know bloody everything,
You probably think you know what I'm going to write,
Because when I start to rhyme,
You barely need any time,
To predict the rhyme up next,
And know every bit of text,
You're always on my mind,
I wonder if you're kind,
I wonder who you are,
When I'm driving in my *bananas*,
Ha, predict that.
Fuck you AI.

# Thank Yous

It's tough to admit for someone in my position. As a future award-winning author, a bit of the magic and aura around my monstrous talent fritters away when I openly claim I couldn't have done it alone. My mind then starts to imagine that maybe I could have and whether it's worth remembering anyone I currently know as I write this. I'm sure I could have done it alone, but ultimately I haven't, so I have some thanking to do.

Musically, Louis Cole and Jamiroquai. I used to be a diehard Oasis fan but after seeing lots of diehard Oasis fans at Knebworth, it put me off of being one. Who knows if I'll return. Jamiroquai's funky songs fuelled lots of walks and exercise sessions that were absolutely necessary to allow my mind the space to create. Louis Cole is just such a cool "dude" and gives me real credibility in regards to my music taste, as well as also being fuel for my moving around. I heard him mention the importance of visual art in his music, which made me realise how important the look of my poems is. I still don't know what my particular "look" is, but I know if I want stuff to work as best it can, it can't look shit. It's probably a bit weird to thank musicians but who's going to stop me?

Now I am going to mention "influences". Before I do, however, I'd like to explain that these people actually all made my life worse in many ways. By being inspired by them, enjoying them, and most of all relating to them, I felt even more out of place in the world of office jobs and it made me feel even more caged and miserable. Thank you all.

John Cooper Clarke helped me realise I could do rhyming poetry and not be an utter knob. His poem "Twat" is a personal favourite and seeing people enjoy it made me think people might enjoy my nonsense one day. Sean Lock and Bob Mortimer, who gave me countless hours of escape from reality, deserve a mention. What wonderful men. Sadly Sean passed before I got to become his best friend. It was a death that makes me feel weird to this day, but I shall not say any more about it. I am convinced he would hate me if I turned his passing into some sort of wet shite. If I ever have the honour of meeting Bob or Sean's ghost, it'd be hard to get across the true sincerity of my thank you and significance of how they've improved my life, but surely getting it down in an official book does the trick, and puts me above everyone else who likes them. I once saw Bob Mortimer outside of an Angelos Epithemiou show but I'm not counting standing five yards behind the back of someone's head as meeting someone.

And lastly, my final influence, your friend and mine, Tim Key. A brilliant, gorgeous man. One of the few people on Earth who can have any length of hair or beard and still look basically the same. Similar to John but to a greater degree, Tim made it feel like it was possible to do what I'm doing, like it was a real thing that can be a profession. A little bit of me hates him because he's so fucking perfect, but I've brushed that part of me aside to do the right thing and acknowledge him. Thank him even. Love him perhaps. Perhaps not though, as to quote Tim directly—love, can be a bit of a fucker.

Now the people I actually know who deserve a thanks. My friends who don't really get it but regardless supported my vision. That's a pretty good test of whether they're your friends, if they don't particularly like what you do but they want it to work for you.

My friends who gave me countless boosts of confidence by laughing or liking something I created. It would have been a nightmare had I had to judge everything on my own. These nosey people gave me honest feedback too, and with them all being quite different, a real sense that I could appeal to different people.

In no particular order, Grandma, Gramps and Nan for all their hard work helping to raise a poet (one of the most difficult jobs on Earth) and seeing how truly fucking special I was even at like three years old. That can be extended to aunts and uncles.

Father, for stepping up numerous times before I even started to write and was being a bit incompetent at life, as well as pushing through his own tough times. He broke a seemingly quite long line of incredibly poor fathers in the family. It's sometimes hard to believe a poet is related in any way to those rotters.

And in a deserved top spot, my mother. An unparalleled strength in the face of everything unfortunate that she's faced. Supportive of me with or without good logic. It's impossible to measure the impact this has had but I'm in a pretty good place to endure life now, and that's the ultimate goal of a parent right? Also, she's made it into a book, so I've given plenty back. My mother got inundated with poems, questions about grammar and had to proofread this book multiple times, so *you* should all thank her too. If it was not for her, this book might not even be readable and I would be sectioned.

# Author Profile

Henry has now turned 30 and is absolutely fine with it. His decision to move back in with his mother is deemed a sensible one, and if anybody questions his credibility as an adult, he reminds them that he adopted a traumatised dog when he lived on his own and nurtured him into society by himself. If this hasn't won them round, he says he lived in Brixton for three years to get some things out of his system and is now "career focused".

His decision to transition his life towards being a poet was met with general acceptance from friends and family, partly due to him being so miserable and hapless in normal jobs, and partly due to the fact that becoming a successful poet allows no room whatsoever for newfound arrogance. If anything, it encourages more people to laugh at him and cast judgement. Nowadays, whenever he has to refer to himself, he usually flaps between "poet" or "artist" or "author", but occasionally says "tortured soul" if the person he is speaking to is unpleasant and he wants to make them vomit. The truth of it all is that each of the labels makes him feel uncomfortable.

On his to-do list for the next 12 months, is to release *The Little Book of Horrid Hopes* and *Humanimals*, start work on another book similar to this one, and for the fourth bullet point he's just written "lady". Three out of four are realistic.

# Please

If you've been able to stomach this book or even managed a smile, would you be up for helping me out by leaving a review? For better or worse, reviews really make a difference and help me to create future books that I hope you'll enjoy. If you can spare a few minutes to leave a review on Amazon, I'd be ever so thankful.

For more, weekly shenanigans, subscribe to my blog -
www.henrymulliganpoet.com

## Publisher Information

Rowanvale Books provides publishing services to independent authors, writers and poets all over the globe. We deliver a personal, honest and efficient service that allows authors to see their work published, while remaining in control of the process and retaining their creativity. By making publishing services available to authors in a cost-effective and ethical way, we at Rowanvale Books hope to ensure that the local, national and international community benefits from a steady stream of good quality literature.

For more information about us, our authors or our publications, please get in touch.

www.rowanvalebooks.com
info@rowanvalebooks.com

Milton Keynes UK
Ingram Content Group UK Ltd.
UKHW051052161123
432674UK00011B/118